C000203809

Murder & Crime
SHEFFIELD

Murder & Crime
SHEFFIELD

MARGARET DRINKALL

The
History
Press

First published 2009

The History Press
The Mill, Brimscombe Port
Stroud, Gloucestershire, GL5 2QG
www.thehistorypress.co.uk

© Margaret Drinkall, 2009

The right of Margaret Drinkall to be identified as the Author
of this work has been asserted in accordance with the
Copyrights, Designs and Patents Act 1988.

All rights reserved. No part of this book may be reprinted
or reproduced or utilised in any form or by any electronic,
mechanical or other means, now known or hereafter invented,
including photocopying and recording, or in any information
storage or retrieval system, without the permission in writing
from the Publishers.
British Library Cataloguing in Publication Data.
A catalogue record for this book is available from the British Library.

ISBN 978 0 7524 5568 6

Typesetting and origination by The History Press
Printed in Great Britain

CONTENTS

ACKNOWLEDGEMENTS

My interest in crime in the Victorian era was awakened by my research for a book on murder and crime in Rotherham. Reading the local newspapers and documents of the period was like being in a time machine, taking me back to a period of brutality and poverty. Not all Sheffield people were criminals, of course, and many people led poor but respectable existences. But it is difficult to resist looking at the criminal element of the city and the hard lives that they often led, knowing thankfully that at the end of the research I can go back to life with my own family and friends. One can't help feeling sorry for some of the people within these pages. Many children at the time were transported for picking pockets or stealing food, but many had no option but to steal to stay alive. Using the *Sheffield & Rotherham Independent* for accounts of the crimes (and for many of the illustrations in this book of the period; for a full list see the Bibliography) I have included snippets of incidents which were happening in the town at the same time as the murderers were committing their crimes. I hope this reflects that most of the citizens of the town showed a curiosity in the events of Sheffield and the country itself. However, my grateful thanks go to the unnamed journalists of the time.

Writing any book is being part of a team and as always the product is the work of many tireless people. I have primarily to thank Cate Ludlow, Helen Bradbury, Nicola Guy and David Lewis from the History Press, all of whom have been incredibly supportive and helpful through the process of writing. I would also like to thank the staff of the Sheffield Local Studies Library and the Sheffield Archives for their unfailing help (and particularly for some of the illustrations which have been made available to me through the Picture Sheffield service). I would urge anyone to make more use of the facilities within the archive and the library service as they are a mine of historical information. I would also like to thank the South Yorkshire Police Service for giving me permission to research the charge books and for permission to reproduce material from the charge books themselves.

I also would like to thank my son, Chris, for his help with the modern photographs of Sheffield as it is today. I hope that when people walk down these streets and roads, where mostly only modern buildings now remain, they will spare a thought for the long-ago tragedies which took place there in the hope that no ghosts still lurk.

INTRODUCTION

Sheffield during the Victorian period was a rapidly expanding industrial town. Its famous industries resulted in the town developing a reputation for being unhealthy and unsanitary, and many of the workshops, factories and warehouses were placed higgledy-piggledy around the homes of the people who worked in them. Only the better-off classes benefited from the booming expansion, allowing them to move out of the centre into the city's more rural suburbs.

The large civic buildings indicated the esteem in which the townspeople held their city. The Cutlers Hall, built in 1832 for the Master Cutlers of the city; the cathedral, which was formerly the parish church and was elevated to cathedral status in 1914, and the founding of the university in 1828 all indicate the Victorians' vision of the importance of their city. But in the underground criminal world of Victorian Sheffield we see a very different picture.

The population of the city exploded during the Industrial Revolution, resulting in the overcrowded tenements with low rents where most working class people were found. The crowded courts and yards were the places where many people lived out their lives, some verging on crime and dishonesty. Punishment for crimes in the Victorian era was, like the lives some of Sheffield's inhabitants led, swift and brutal, and the road to the scaffold was inexorable. Criminals of the town who were arrested would find themselves at the Town Hall in Castle Street, which held the police offices and the town cells. This was the place where many of the murderers in this book would find themselves. When a dead body was found, the first formal procedure was the holding of an inquest where, with some notable exceptions, the accused appeared. Inquests were often held at the nearest public house to where the body was found and the jury would inspect the body before the inquest. The jury's duty was not to judge whether the accused person was guilty or not, but purely to establish the cause of death. If the verdict was one of 'guilty' they would be sent to the Assizes in Leeds, York and latterly Wakefield, where they would be tried by a judge. If their guilt was proven they would be sentenced to death. During this period, the nation's prisons were

Industrial Sheffield. (Reproduced courtesy of Picture Sheffield)

Sheffield Cutlers Hall. (Chris Drinkall)

Sheffield Cathedral. (Chris Drinkall)

The Town Hall where prisoners were held in the cells. (Reproduced courtesy of Picture Sheffield)

A typical street in Sheffield during the Victorian Era. (Reproduced courtesy of Picture Sheffield)

becoming overcrowded and an alternative method of punishment was required to hold prisoners. Hulks of ships were used to contain prisoners until sufficient numbers could be transported to Australia and Tasmania.

Penal transportation was an alternative to imprisonment and capital punishment, and some of the cases in this book suffered such a fate. According to J.P. Bean's book *Crime in Sheffield*, in 1819 a total of 164 felons (including seven capital offences) were transported, this figure rising to 346 in 1845. The life of a transported criminal was no sinecure. They would be condemned to work in chain gangs, building roads and performing other heavy, labour-intensive work. Women would be used as domestic labour for the term of their service.

These then are the stories behind the crimes. One thing is for certain: the wicked lives these characters led, and the punishment they received, indicate that some of the murderers in this book exchanged one brutal existence for another.

Chapter One

———◈◈◈———

The Body in the Street

In January 1841, Sheffield was reeling from the effects of a storm which hit the town between 3 a.m. and 4 p.m. on Sunday the 3rd. The storm – which consisted of hail, rain, sleet and snow – was accompanied by thunder and lightning. It would seem that the elements were conspiring against the population of the town, for the citizens awoke on the morning of 9 January to find a dense fog, of a type rarely seen today, hanging over the streets and roads of the city. The cold weather in Sheffield continued and, on the night of 23 January 1841, a flurry of snow collected on a small mound – a body which had been left out on the street. Marks in the surrounding snow suggested that the death had not been an accident.

During this period the streets of Sheffield were patrolled by constables and nightwatchmen. There had been a disturbance at the house of George Reaney of Thomas Street the night before, but the neighbours said that the ruckus was nothing new; Saturday nights in that area often resounded with the sounds of screaming wives, beaten by their dissolute husbands, and drunken shouts from couples arguing after a long night in the public houses of the town. A neighbour, one Samuel Benson of 65 Thomas Street, thought he heard a noise at about 1 p.m. on the Sunday morning; he suspected someone was breaking down the door of the neighbouring house. However, he was used to such noises and thought that his neighbour had returned home from a drunken spree. He therefore tried to ignore the sounds and to get back to sleep – though he heard female voices and thought he heard one say to the other, 'Poor George!'. About 1.30 a.m. he got out of bed to look out of the window. He could still hear voices at George's front door, but the voices were so low that he couldn't make out what they were saying. Even later, he recalled hearing the sound of women going up and down the street. He eventually fell asleep – only to be woken at 4.30 a.m. by the nightwatchman, Jonathan Lawton, calling for help, shouting that he had found a dead man in the street below.

Lawton admitted that when he saw the body he thought it was a sleeping drunk; he went over to wake him up. He noted that although the man was stiff he wasn't

Sheffield police uniforms of 1890. (Reproduced courtesy of Picture Sheffield)

particularly cold, which was surprising as the weather was cold enough to snow. The body was laid out in the middle of the road, face down, with arms outstretched. The unknown man was aged about forty and there was much disfigurement of his face (which looked as if it had taken quite a heavy beating). There had been a light scattering of snow in the night, which had started to fall around 4 p.m., and the tracks indicated that the man had been dragged to the middle of the street at this point. There were footprints in the snow leading from George's house to the body, as well as drops of blood. The dead man was not wearing a hat and his coat had been nearly dragged off as he had been pulled over the ground. He was lying in a pool of blood.

Lawton had difficulty seeing the body as his own light had been blown out by the wind, so he used the rattle provided for him to summon help; another watchman, James Hanley, soon arrived. Lawton told him that he felt that the man had lain there all night, but Hanley disagreed – he felt the evidence of the snow showed that the body had not been there for any length of time. Together, the two watchmen knocked on the door of Reaney's house, but no one answered. At this point they called out to the neighbours to see if there had been any disturbances. The neighbour on the other side of George Reaney's house, John Chapman, said that he too had heard noises. He added that he thought he heard someone screaming 'Thou will no more', but he wasn't sure whose voice he had heard. He also confirmed that it was not uncommon to hear noises from next door, 'Especially on a Saturday night', and so, thinking no more about it, he too went back to sleep. Samuel Benson and two others helped the nightwatchmen to move the body to the nearby Peacock Tavern. The two neighbours asked the watchmen if they had patrolled the streets that night, and if so, how they had possibly missed a dead body stretched out in the middle of the street for up to three hours? The watchmen told them that they had done their duty, and that the body was not seen until 4.30 a.m. when it was found by Lawton.

At 6 a.m. Police Constable William Drake appeared on the scene and immediately took charge. He had been called by a woman about 5 a.m. and had gone to view the body at the Peacock Tavern. However, the corpse's face was so badly disfigured he could not say with certainty who the dead man was. Arrangements were accordingly made to wash the corpse's face in the hopes that this would make identification possible. Whilst this was being done, Drake examined the spot where the body had been found and found bloodstains in the snow. He also went to Reaney's house – and after knocking and gaining no reply, he broke the door down and entered. Inside he found blood on the floor, a smashed jug placed on the sink and a bloody cloth (which looked like it had been used in an attempt to mop up the blood). A mahogany card

Thomas Street as it looks today. (Chris Drinkall)

have some ale, and witness then endea-
ke peace, but the deceased would not.—
nt on to Hyde Park, and got into a field.
the prisoner wanted their shopmates to
out they all refused. The parties were
minutes before they could get anybody to
and they then said if they could get no
would trip one another up. They then
coming up, and the deceased and pri-
to ask if any one would second them,
efused. After a time the prisoners Mor-
k came up; and the former seconded
the latter the deceased. The parties be-
and fought for more than an hour. They
thirty rounds, and at length Ghaloghy
ry severe blow on the side. Witness went
ould make it up, but the deceased re-
id he would blacken Dawson's other eye.
und, Dawson being very near completely
eceased a violent blow at the back of the
the fell and lay on the ground in a state
y; he vomited soon afterwards; witness
a doctor; in the course of the battle
both the seconds to make it up several
ey refused, and called "time." ....Cross-
Vas not more partial to the deceased be-
e from the same country. Never could
he deceased's company, he was so quarrel
cross-examination brought out the facts
ased was the most wishful to fight; that
willing, and even wishful for peace; and
was not at first very wishful to act as se-
deceased provoked Dawson to fight, and
expert and stronger of the two; Dawson
urgeon to be sent for when the deceased
last round.
ith, the next witness, was present at the
roborated the evidence of the former wit-
le deceased to the Infirmary....Cross-
aw the deceased throw up his hat as a
Dawson.
itfield, who was also present at the fight,
evidence.
n Overend, senior surgeon of the Shef-
ry, was called in to attend the deceased
the evening; he was suffering from com-
he brain, caused from external injuries;
veral marks on the neck and sides of the
d the same night at about a quarter before
ined the body, and attributed his death
of one of the blood vessels of the brain,
it be caused by a blow or a heavy fall....
ued: There was no mark corresponding

The elder prisoner put several questions to the boy
Feenely, who was the witness, to shew that he had
no connexion with the young prisoner and Crowdie.
The boy replied that the younger prisoner and Crowdie were away from himself and the elder prisoner
for weeks together, and that the elder prisoner never
ill-treated the boy, but on one or two occasions wished the younger prisoner to treat him better.
Mr. Baron Rolfe summed up. He intimated that
there was no case against the elder prisoner. The
charge against the younger prisoner was for killing
and slaying, but the boy did not appear to have died
from any bruises received. It was competent for
them, if they did not convict of manslaughter, to convict him on the charge of assault.
The Jury returned a verdict of Guilty of an assault against the younger prisoner; and of Not
Guilty against the elder prisoner.
Baron Rolfe said, that though he believed the
death of the poor boy had not been caused by ill
usage, yet there could be no doubt that the younger
prisoner had treated him with gross brutality, and for
the protection of poor unoffending children, he felt
it his duty to sentence him to be imprisoned for the
term of one year.
MANSLAUGHTER AT SHEFFIELD.
GEORGE REANEY (35), was charged with the
manslaughter of George Belk, at Sheffield. Mr.
WORTLEY and Mr. OVEREND were for the prosecution; Sir G. LEWIN defended the prisoner.
Mr. Wortley, for the prosecution, stated the cir-
stances as follows:—On the morning of Sunday, the
24th January last, about one o'clock, a considerable
noise was heard by the neighbours of the prisoner,
who lived in Thomas street, Sheffield, apparently pro-
ceeding from his house, and as though there was some
fighting going on. It was not, however, so loud as to
induce them to make any inquiry. In the morning,
the dead body of a man was found lying in the street,
by a policeman, while passing the prisoner's door.
The prisoner was apprehended at his mother's house,
by a police officer of the name of Drake. Before the
officer could tell him the charge against him, he acknowledged that he had killed the man, and voluntarily made a statement that he went home about one
o'clock on Sunday morning in liquor, and on going
into the house he heard voices, one of which was the
voice of his wife, and the other that of a man. He
heard his wife say, " Give over, give over, my husband
will be coming." The prisoner burst into the room;
there was no light in it, and without knowing who he
was, he seized hold of the deceased, upon whom he
immediately commenced a violent attack. A struggle
ensued, and the deceased was got under by the pri-

foot, which had a hollow in the middle
The hat picked up by the prosecutor w
sworn to have belonged to Terry, having
to him about four months previously.
The Jury acquitted Fieldhouse; the o
er Terry was found Guilty.—To be in
hard labour for six calendar months.
RICHARD SPEIGHT (46,) was cl
having, at Selby, feloniously embezzled
of money received by him as clerk to
Fothergill, attorney, on account of the B
and Skyrack Court of Requests.—Si
LEWIN and Mr. HALL were for the
Mr. BLISS defended the prisoner.—Th
was a clerk in the service of Mr. Fothe
agent to Mr. Clark, the clerk to the B
and Skyrack Court of Requests. The d
to receive various sums from parties w
gants in the court, and it was his dut
these sums to the managing clerk. O
July he received a sum of £1. 1s. 9d. f
named Rawlinson, and on the 10th of S
received 4s. from a person of the name
—neither of which sums he had account
defence was that sums in question had l
during a press of business, and that t
had omitted to pay them, not from a
intention, but from inadvertence and n
Guilty.
The prisoner was then arraigned on
dictment, charging him with having fe
bezzled the sum of £1, received by hi
Mr. Mark Fothergill, attorney, on a
Barkston Ash and Skyrack Court of R
the 9th of March the prisoner had rec
of £1. 9s. 8d. from a person named Al
and had only paid 9s. 8d., leaving a l
unaccounted for.—The defence was t
sum had been paid over.—Not Guilty.
GEORGE FIRTH (25,) JOSEPH
(27,) and HENRY HARGREAVE
charged with feloniously stealing 120 p
of lambs wool, from the dwelling-hou
Brook, of Lindley, near Huddersfield
LEY was for the prosecution; Mr. WILL
the prisoners.—The prisoners were all
——They were then arraigned on a
ment, but the evidence of the receiver
roborated, they were acquitted.—The e
the first indictment was deferred.
MAGISTRATES' ROO
SATURDAY.—Several prisoners
fore Mr. ARMSTRONG, but the case
devoid of interest.

George Reaney's trial. (*Sheffield & Rotherham Independent*, 20 March 1841)

table was smashed to smithereens near the foot of the stairs. Going upstairs he found a broken chair, but the bed was made and looked like it had been undisturbed. There was no one in the house.

He went back to the Peacock Tavern and recognised the newly washed body as being that of George Belk, an edge-tool maker employed by Messrs S. Newbould & Co. Recognizing that he could go no further until he had spoken to Reaney, he made enquiries as to his whereabouts. He was told that Mrs Reaney's sister, widow Mary Wilson, lived in Gaol Lane, so he accordingly made his way there. The door was opened by Mary. Drake asked for George Reaney – but before he could say any more, Reaney himself came to the door and told him, 'I was coming to deliver myself up to you. I have murdered a man!' Drake asked George to accompany him to the Town Hall for further questioning, the two men accompanied on their journey by Reaney's wife and her sister. On the way Reaney confessed to Drake, 'It is perfectly right…

I am very sorry for it. I did not think I was going to that extent'. At the Town Hall he made a statement and was charged with the offence. Incredibly, up to that point it seems that Reaney had no idea who he had killed. When told who the victim was he stated, 'Good God, is that the man? No person was a better friend than George Belk and me!'

Reaney told Drake that he and his wife had been married quite happily for almost eleven years. He described returning home the previous night, little expecting the drama which was about to unfold. He had arrived home about 1 a.m., and, as was his custom, he had brought some haddock for supper. He was therefore astonished to find the house in darkness. As he approached, he heard his wife's voice saying to someone, 'Now don't, give over, for I expect my master home directly'. Opening the door, he entered the house and could just make out the outline of two people: his wife and another man. Reaney felt that he had interrupted some kind of sexual encounter and grabbed the man by the neck. He smashed the man repeatedly in the face with his other hand. Reaney told the inquest that he had no intention of killing the man; he just wanted to give him a sound thrashing and throw him out of the house. The pair struggled and they fell onto the card table, which broke beneath their combined weight. He told Drake that at this point he was on top of the man, who he was still holding by the neck. The unfortunate Belk suddenly made a gurgling noise and lay still, and Reaney realized that he was dead.

In his statement Reaney said that the house was so dark that he could not see the deceased man's face. He asked his wife to get a candle, but as she was sobbing hysterically he went to a neighbour's house instead and asked him for a candle. The neighbour, James Crawshaw, saw the state Reaney was in, and Reaney confessed that he had killed a man. Crawshaw told the jury that he 'gave him two Lucifer's [matches]' – and incredibly that he then went back to bed! He only saw the body in the street the following morning. Back at the house, the couple lit a candle and looked closer at the man on the floor. It seems that even in the candlelight he had not recognised the man he had killed (no doubt because Belk's face was covered in blood). He then ran out of the house.

In his distressed state he went to his parents' house and told them what had happened. His parents were distraught when he told them that he was about to give himself up, but his mother asked him to 'wait a while'. They talked about what had happened and they knew that he could be hung for this night's work. Uanble to believe he had killed the man, Reaney thought he would go back home and see if the man was really dead, telling his parents that 'he would be back within the hour'. He told them that if the man was dead that he would be giving himself up to the Town Hall, but instead of going directly home he went to Mary Wilson's house and asked his wife to confirm that the man was really dead. She admitted that he was. As they stood there considering the implications of the night's work, there was a knock on the door and there stood Constable Drake.

The constable next wanted to take statements from the two women, Jane Reaney and Mary Wilson, who appeared to have had an equally eventful night. It seems that both women had gone out for a drink up 'the Moor' where they met Belk, who Jane

The Pump Tavern, where Jane Reaney and Mary Wilson went for a drink with George Belk. (Reproduced courtesy of Picture Sheffield)

had known for about three years. He invited both women for a drink in the Anvil public house, where he bought them two drinks each. They then went to the Pump Tavern – where things began to get out of hand. Within minutes Belk was trying to kiss Jane – 'pulling her about', as Mary put it. She told him to desist or she would buy her own drinks; he said he wanted to go home with her, but she told him that he couldn't as her husband was due home for his supper. According to Mary, they left him at the door of the Pump Tavern and walked home.

However, Jane Reaney had other ideas. After her sister bade her goodnight, she went back to the Anvil public house. There she saw a young man, James Jackson, aged eleven, going into the pub to get some gin for his mother. She asked him to ask Belk to come outside as she wanted to talk to him. However, when he returned it transpired that Belk had not been seen in the pub for the last two hours. She appeared quite distressed at this news and wrung her hands, saying, 'Oh dear, oh dear'. Belk, in the meantime, had gone to Mary Wilson's house to get some more alcohol. She told him to go home as he had had enough. Wilson described the last time she saw him, weaving unsteadily up Gaol Lane.

When Jane Reaney gave evidence at the inquest held at the Peacock Tavern on Monday 25 January, she described how she had arrived home after the drinks with Belk and gone about her household chores. After some time, she sat down by the fire and fell asleep. When she awoke the house was in darkness, the fire burning very low and the candle gone out. She heard someone walk in the door and called, 'Who is it?'

Belk answered, 'It's me, my lass… Is George home?'

She replied, 'No, mester, do go out, do go out, I expect my husband home any minute'.

With that he began pulling on her gown, despite her telling him to desist. Belk was still pulling at her gown when, to her horror, she heard her husband at the door. He came in, shouting, 'What are you doing with my wife at this time of night, you rogue?' She heard them struggle and they both fell on the floor. She thought she heard a groan. After what seemed like a very short struggle, Reaney said to her, 'Surely I have not killed him?' They got a light – and sure enough, Belk looked dead. Also refusing to accept that Belk was dead, she went to her sister's house and asked her to come back with her to find out whether Belk was dead or not, but her sister was frightened. At some point it was decided – by whom, we do not know – that the body would have to be put outside in the street. (Whether they thought it would be assumed that he had died in an accident is unknown, but we do know that as he was a heavy-set man they were unable to move him by themselves.) The pair then went to the house in Gaol Lane of another widow, Mary Bailey, and offered her a shilling to come back to the house and find out if the man was dead and to help get him out of the house. Bailey refused, despite an increased offer of 2s. Mary Bailey told the coroner that she was tempted as she had a large family, but she had eventually refused, stating that she 'Would not go for a thousand shillings'. Jane said that 'It was alright' as no one knew about what had happened, at which point Mary Bailey piously – and rather unhelpfully – added that 'God above knows', and refused point blank to help. It was reported that Jane Reaney was crying piteously as she turned away from the house.

The next to give his evidence was the nightwatchman, Lawton. His evidence was quite confusing, and he contradicted himself on many occasions. He stated to the coroner, Mr T. Badger Esq., that he had patrolled his beat as usual about 1 a.m. or 2 a.m. and there was no sign or sounds of any disturbance in Thomas Street. He went up the street again about 2 a.m. or 3 a.m. and there was no corpse in the street at that time. The first time he saw the body was at 4.30 a.m. when he called for help. A juror questioned him as to whether nightwatchmen had been instructed to interfere if there was a domestic argument taking place whilst they were on patrol. Lawton replied that they would not interfere in a row in a private house unless they were called upon, or heard a cry of 'murder' shouted. He testified to the fact that he had not seen any women in the streets that evening. Samuel Benson was then questioned about hearing women pacing the streets between 1 a.m. and 2 a.m. that morning. But Lawton denied once more that he had seen any women that night.

Other witnesses were heard and the inquest ran late. By 9.30 p.m. it was agreed that the inquest, which was to be moved to the Town Hall, be adjourned until the following morning, Thursday 28 January. At this adjourned inquest James Crawshaw gave his evidence. He bluntly told the coroner and the jury that he had heard that Jane Reaney was known to be a 'dissolute woman'. The surgeon, Dr James Walker, who completed the post-mortem, stated that he found multiple bruises on the body of George Belk.

There were several abrasions of the skin on the deceased and discoloration at the throat where there had been a compression of the larynx. There were also small wounds around the mouth of the dead man. In addition it appeared that his heart was not healthy and the surgeon admitted that this could have contributed to the man's death. The coroner summed up the case and told the jury that they had to decide whether this case was one of murder or manslaughter. He told them that in 1835 a judge named Baron Parks had laid down that when a husband killed an adulterous wife in the act of adultery, it was manslaughter if he saw it with his own eyes, a term known in law as 'ocular demonstration of the fact'. Because of the darkness of the house and by the prisoner's own admission that he saw very little in the dark, then the jury must decide whether or not there was enough provocation to cause him to kill Belk in 'a reasonable passion'. If they felt that he had hesitated or that there had been a 'cooling off period' then they had to bring in a verdict of wilful murder. The jury brought in a verdict of manslaughter and Reaney was sent to Leeds for his trial. Mrs Jane Reaney was dismissed from the court with a severe reprimand, the coroner pointing out that she could have got rid of Belk if she really wanted to by crying out. Combined with the fact that she had gone to the Anvil public house looking for Belk, he felt these facts indicated that her own part in the matter could not be so easily dismissed.

The trial of George Reaney took place on 20 March 1841. After hearing all the evidence, the defence, QC Sir G. Lewin, dwelt on the fact that the surgeon had stated that Belk was not in the best state of health and could not truthfully say that the violence of the deceased's own efforts might not have contributed to his death. He stated 'the circumstances of the case are such as to call for the sympathy of every one who heard them'. The judge in directing the jury told them that 'he was sure the jury would give to the prisoner the benefits of all those probabilities as to the cause of death'. In a very short time the jury returned the verdict which was 'not guilty', and George Reaney walked from the dock a free man.

It would seem that this murder was committed in a place where it was common practice to hear screams, thumps and bangs in the night. The lack of interest shown by the witnesses testifies that the night of 23 January 1841 was no different to other nights when arguments took place. No doubt the daytime would have witnessed equal scenes of violence and abuse between men and women. The next case which demonstates this took place in Red Croft, where a screaming harridan caused a man's death in a place which appeared to be dominated by thieves and murderers...

Chapter Two

—◆—

Manslaughter at Red Croft

In November 1841 the biggest news in the town was the birth of the Prince of Wales to Queen Victoria. Albert Edward (known as Bertie) was born on 9 November and he was the longest-serving Prince of Wales, his name being synonymous with the decadent lifestyle to which he dedicated most of his life. Nevertheless he was the first child to Queen Victoria and Prince Albert and no doubt the people of the town would have joined in the many celebrations of the birth of the heir to the British throne.

The lives of many of the people of Sheffield in 1841 could have no comparison with that of the Royal Family. No doubt there were many respectable families who chose to emulate the highest family in the land, but many more lived lives of abuse and criminal activity. Red Croft on Pinfold Street was notorious as a place where thieves and murderers collected. In the case that follows, one local reporter stated sanctimoniously that 'the whole of the parties are of the lowest character'. In 1841 the brothel on Red Croft did plenty of business, and the fact that it could be accessed from the back ensured anonymity for most of its customers. The case began in November 1841 at the house of Mr Bradbury of Heeley. The building had been broken into and a large amount of alcohol stolen. The booty consisted of fifteen gallons of whisky in quart bottles and six dozen bottles each of port and sherry. The division of these stolen goods was to result in one of the thieves murdering the other...

On Sunday 7 November the weather was mild enough for the time of the year to have some of the residents of Red Croft taking the air at about 11.45 a.m. Henry Rodgers, aged thirty-two, woke and went to have breakfast with his wife; however, due to the absence of her father, she was intent on having breakfast with her mother. Rodgers had long ago decided not to argue with his wife – who could be very vocal in her demands – and so after breakfast he went upstairs to his workroom, which was in the garret. He was a shoemaker by trade and often worked in his garret, but he was planning to read rather than work this morning. He had recently obtained a book published in Edinburgh which outlined the workings of the steam engine. However, he had only turned a couple of pages when he was disturbed by his daughter shouting to him. He looked out of the garret window and saw William Stringer, aged twenty-seven, passing the back way towards the local brothel, which was owned by Mr Shemeld and his wife. Rodgers took some tobacco and went back to his book.

Outside, groups of neighbours were gathered, and Stringer was quietly talking to another unnamed man, when a screeching woman disturbed their peace. She was Elizabeth, the wife of Henry Rodgers, and she was well-known in the district to be both physically and verbally abusive. She accused Stringer of being a 'bully and a prig' and claimed 'that he never did anything but get his money by prigging or stealing'. He called her 'a lousy bitch' and said that 'if she did not go home he would make her'. She challenged him to hit her – and he did.

One of the neighbours, a man called George Ashton Bailey, was sitting in his kitchen and at about a minute to twelve o'clock he heard a noise in the croft. He went outside to investigate, and appeared just in time to see Elizabeth Rodgers lash out at Stringer. She called him a 'skulking thief' and struck him on the face several times with her hands, shouting abuse at him. He retaliated by striking her with his fists and knocking her to the ground. He then called her a 'bloody whore' and said that he could prove that she had 'been with him many times'. She got up again and ran to her house to call her husband – who calmly opened the window of the garret and shouted at her to hold her peace. She told him that Stringer was telling their neighbours that he had been intimate with her on many occasions. Her husband told her to come inside, and that Stringer was just being malicious, but she angrily retaliated that if he would not defend her she would do it for herself and she rushed back to where Stringer was still standing.

At this point her mother intervened and tried to pull her daughter away from Stringer, but she continued abusing him. By this time the sound of raised voices and the insults being exchanged caused many of the residents to come out of their houses. Some of them shouted at Rodgers to defend his wife, calling out to him that Stringer was killing poor Bess. Rodgers put his book down, and, picking up the knife which he used in his trade of shoemaking, he went outside. Rodgers didn't speak directly to Stringer, but when Stringer saw that he had a knife in his hand he knelt down to pick up part of a brick with which to defend himself. Rodgers rushed at him and stabbed him in the bottom of his stomach and then at one side of the neck and then the other. The wound in his belly was so bad that part of his intestines began slipping out, and he fell to the ground clutching his stomach. The blood was gushing out of him, and Bailey went to fetch a doctor.

By now the neighbours were gathering around the injured man. George Jenkinson, picked up Stringer's hat, which had been knocked off in the struggle, and he took off Stringer's neckerchief to staunch the blood which was by now gushing out of his neck. Stringer pressed the neckerchief to the wound in his throat. John Smith, a knife grinder of nearby Shemeld Croft, said that he had tried to get the knife off Rodgers, but he threatened that he would 'do the same to him'. Rodgers finally managed to get his wife under control and with her mother went back to his own home, which was about twenty yards from where the incident had taken place. Entering the house, they shut the door and the victim was carried to his own house on Red Croft.

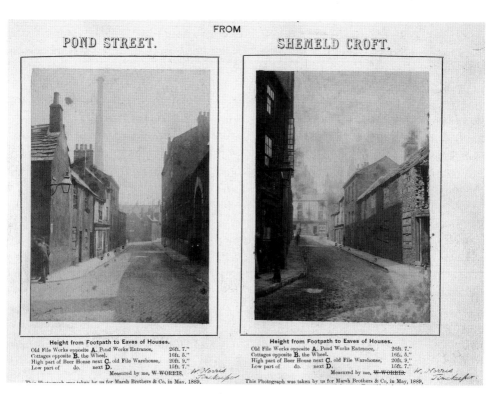

FROM

POND STREET.　　　　　SHEMELD CROFT.

Height from Footpath to Eaves of Houses.

Old File Works opposite **A**. Pond Works Entrance,	26ft. 7."
Cottages opposite **B**. the Wheel.	16ft. 5."
High part of Beer House next **C**. old File Warehouse,	20ft. 9."
Low part of do. next **D**.	15ft. 7."

Measured by me, W. WORRIS.　W. Norris
Tin Keeper

This Photograph was taken by us for Marsh Brothers & Co. in May, 1889.

Height from Footpath to Eaves of Houses.

Old File Works opposite **A**. Pond Works Entrance,	26ft. 7."
Cottages opposite **B**. the Wheel.	16ft. 5."
High part of Beer House next **C**. old File Warehouse,	20ft. 9."
Low part of do. next **D**.	15ft. 7."

Measured by me, W. WORRIS.　W. Norris
Tin Keeper

This Photograph was taken by us for Marsh Brothers & Co. in May, 1889.

Pond Street and Shemeld Croft, 1880. (Reproduced courtesy of Picture Sheffield)

The surgeon, a Mr Turton who had a surgery in Townsend Street, went to Stringer's house with his assistant. The two bound up the man's injuries as best as they could, but it was obvious that his wounds were so severe that he would not recover, and a police constable was sent for. Constable James Maxwell (No. 6 of the Sheffield Police Force) was patrolling his beat in West Street and had almost reached the top of Church Street when he was hailed by George Ashton. As a consequence of Ashton's information he took a watchman with him to Rodgers' house, where he interviewed Elizabeth Rodgers, her mother and other neighbours waiting in the house. He also spoke to a neighbour, Mrs Mary Ann Andrews, who told him that Stringer had the night before gone to Rodgers' house – where there had been a quarrel about the division of the spoils from a robbery. These spoils were none other than the alcohol taken from Mr Bradbury's house.

Stringer was angry that Rodgers has sold the stolen alcohol without consulting him and went to Rodgers' house to demand his share of the money. That was the cause of the argument between Stringer and Elizabeth the next day. Crucially, Andrews told the constable that she saw Rodgers come out of the house not carrying anything, but, witnessing the struggle between his wife and Stringer at the top of the street, he went back into the house for his knife. The knife was described as having a long handle and a short blade. She described how he went towards Stringer with the knife held in his hand facing backwards. Andrews said that she shouted to Stringer to be careful, as Rodgers had got a knife, which he then tried to hide by pushing the knife up his shirtsleeves. She stated that he was muttering, 'I mean it, I'll do it'.

Another neighbour, one Thomas Mason, also a shoemaker by trade, corroborated her story saying that he had seen other suspicious characters in Rodgers' house. He knew that there had been a robbery and that Rodgers was expecting to be apprehended for it. Sarah Palmer, wife of John Palmer, stated to the constable that both men appeared to be sober and that several people had been in the croft that morning. Yet, despite the profusion of people who witnessed the attack, no one had intervened or tried to stop the murder from happening.

Constable Maxwell went back to Rodgers' house to interview him, and went up to the garret, where he found him. Maxwell said to him, 'You have made a pretty job of it; you have nearly killed a man'. Rodgers replied that 'it was no more than he intended to do to me. He had a knife last night and would have done the same for me'. Maxwell asked him where the knife was and Rodgers pointed to a shoemaker's seat, indicating a knife which lay there. He stated that it was the knife he had attacked Stringer with. The knife still had blood on it. The constable told Rodgers that he was going to arrest him and they set off to walk to the Town Hall. During the walk, Rodgers told the constable that 'he should have served him thus long since', but he did not elaborate as to the reasons why. On arriving there he was handed over to and charged by Superintendent Thomas Raynor, who took possession of the knife. Rodgers then made a statement that Stringer had ill-used his wife and struck her, giving her two black eyes. She had called to him and in the heat of passion he had snatched up the knife and gone to help her. Rodgers denied going back into the house for the knife.

At this point, due to the victim being to close to death, a magistrate's clerk, Thomas Thorpe, was sent to the house to take the man's dying deposition. It was important that the dying man was made aware that he was close to his end, to emphasise that the statement he would make would be the truth. Stringer confirmed this, saying that he did not think that he would get well and he expected before long to meet his Maker. Despite the gravity of the situation, Stringer was not about to admit to the robbery, as he told the clerk that the quarrel was about the state in which he had left the lodgings of Rodgers (the two had previously shared lodgings). The clerk wrote down his deposition and then Stringer signed it with a cross. After stating his name and his address, he said:

I am 25 years of age. I used to lodge with Henry Rodgers and I left his house filthy about two months since. I met Rodgers' wife this morning and we began quarrelling about it. She gave me a shove and I shoved her back and she went to fetch her husband. I saw that he had a knife and stooped to pick up a stone but before I could pick it up, he stabbed me in the groin, the neck, first one side and then the other. We had never quarreled before him telling me off about the filth. I have never spoken to Rodgers this seven weeks since. I do not say anything out of malice to Rodgers: I bear him none. If I could be better tomorrow I would forgive him what he has done.

The statement was witnessed by Superintendent Raynor and the clerk and signed by Raynor 'in the presence of us this 7th November 1841 between the hours of 10–11 p.m.'. Stringer was attended by the surgeon Mr Turton and his assistant, who both knew that he would not have more than a few hours to live. Stringer, who was unmarried, died in the company of his cousin, Elizabeth Bishop of Newfield Bridgehouses, at 11.45 a.m. the next day.

Raynor then informed Rodgers, who was held in the Town Hall cells, that Stringer had died earlier that day and told him that he was now facing a murder charge. Rodgers told the superintendent that he was sorry that Stringer was dead as he bore no malice against him and that the crime had been committed in the heat of passion.

The inquest was held at the Town Hall on Tuesday 9 November before the coroner, Mr Thomas Badger. A local reporter said that because of the interest in the case the room was packed with people. Mr Badger opened the inquest by saying that he was determined to ensure that stabbing cases such as this were dealt with most severely, as 'there had been too many of these cases in front of him at this present time'.

He heard evidence given by the surgeon, Mr Turton, who had completed the post-mortem with two other surgeons, Mr Henry Jackson and Mr Edward Harrison. Turton stated that the brain, chest and viscera of the deceased were very healthy. The wound in the groin had been inflicted with 'an inward and upward motion towards the naval'. In opening the cavity of the abdomen he had found much fluid and blood. On the left side of the neck the wound was 1 ¼in in length, and on the right side ¾in. The knife had lacerated large arteries and divided some of the muscles. He concluded that Stringer's death was due to the serious wounds penetrating the belly and cutting the intestines, and the consequent loss of blood.

After listening to all the evidence and after the transcriptions had been made, Rodgers was brought up into the court and the statements were read out to him. The coroner cautioned him that he needn't say anything which might incriminate himself, but if he did it would be taken down and might be used in evidence against him. But rather than remain silent he chose to make a statement outlining the facts. He described how he had found his wife bleeding from the mouth following the attack; the right side of her face was bruised and she had a lump the size of a small egg on her chin. Both she and his daughter were crying, and, incensed with rage, he had run up to Stringer and struck him. He was unable to say where he struck him. He stated that 'the police came and I gave them the knife'.

The coroner, after hearing all the evidence, summed up the case for the jury and explained the difference between murder and manslaughter. He told them that if a person took a weapon with the express intention of killing someone with it, it is murder. When the prisoner went out as a consequence of repeated cries from his wife and the neighbours and, in the heat of the moment, seized the knife, then provocation would be enough to reduce the crime to manslaughter. He went on:

> The prisoner has in his statement made clear that he did not go out until repeatedly called and he has said that he had no malice towards Stringer. However if the statement of Mrs Andrews was to be believed even though no one else has corroborated her statement, that Rodgers had

gone back in for the knife, this would indicate a pause for thought and it would therefore be a case of murder.

The court was cleared until the jury reached their verdict – which was that Rodgers was guilty of manslaughter. The coroner committed him to York for the Spring Assizes and stated that he hoped the judge would make an example of cowardly stabbing cases as there had been so many in Sheffield recently, adding that 'it was such an un-English crime'.

At the Assizes, which were heard on 26 March 1842, the deliberations were mostly about whether the jury felt that this was a case of manslaughter or murder. Mrs Andrews had by this time changed her statement, saying that Rodgers had closed the door after himself, did not go back inside the house again and that the knife was already in his hand. But the prosecution, in their summing up, felt that when the accused tried to hide the knife after Mrs Andrews shouted a warning to the deceased, it indicated 'a proof of malice aforethought'. If the jury believed that he was determined to commit murder, they must find him guilty of the capital offence. The defence tried to prove provocation, citing the attack upon his wife and the shouts of the neighbours and arguing that they were enough to ensure the verdict of manslaughter. The crime had been committed in broad daylight with plenty of witnesses and therefore it could be said that there was no intention to get away with the act and therefore no malice was intended. After a deliberation of two hours, the jury returned with a verdict of manslaughter. The judge adjourned sentencing the prisoner and it was the following week before Rodgers heard that he was to be transported for seven years.

There can be little doubt that the act was committed in the heat of the moment and that certain facts were not brought to the jury's attention. The details that both men were criminals recently involved in a robbery would have done little for their cause. Indeed, the coroner's words indicate that stabbing was a common crime in the city of Sheffield at that time. Another stabbing crime, which was clearly unpremeditated and yet still resulted in the loss of life for a young man, happened on Monday 15 March 1856, when a petty argument ended up in murder.

Chapter Three

⇒◆⇐

Death of 'America'

William Ibbotson, aged eighteen, was 'stepping out' with Alice Farr of Smithfield. As sometimes happens in these cases, she had called him some names, as a result of which he hit her. Another young man, called John Pinder, decided that he would revenge Miss Farr's attack (and perhaps get into her good books as a result...). He let it be known that if he saw Ibbotson around he would chastise him for his cowardly behaviour towards the girl – and then took his plan one step further by deciding to ambush him near to the place where he lived. He took some friends along with him to make sure that he had an appreciative audience. Ibbotson, otherwise known as 'America' since his parents had gone out to the New World to live, was living with his grandmother on Acorn Street, Shalesmoor. Accordingly Pinder, aged eighteen, was accompanied by Mary Ann Thompson, aged sixteen, Mary Ann Igge, aged fourteen, and Charles Revill, aged seventeen. The party went to Acorn Street at 5.30 p.m. and hid in a passage near to where Ibbotson lived.

When Pinder saw him coming he rushed out and hit him in the face. Ibbotson was carrying a 'stick of scissors' for a friend and lashed out at Pinder with the stick. One of the pairs of scissors on the stick pierced the side of Pinder's head at the left temple, entering the brain. Pinder staggered to the centre of the road, where he fell down insensible. One of the witnesses gave evidence at the inquest held on the body of John Pinder on Wednesday 17 March. Mary Ann Thompson, who lived on School Croft, worked with Pinder at the warehouse of Mr Hancock, cutlery manufacturer, on Pea Croft. She told the jury that she had heard the deceased threaten to beat Ibbotson and before they all headed to Acorn Street had asked Pinder if he intended to hit him. Pinder replied that he and Revill wouldn't hurt him. She said that after the attack Revill and another man helped to pick the body up and take it into the house of Ibbotson's grandmother.

The next witness obviously shocked the coroner and the jury to the core when he revealed that he had never said prayers or been to church, chapel or school in his life. Charles Revill of Edward Street told the shocked assembled persons that he did

Edward Street as it looks today, where witness Charles Revill lived. (Chris Drinkall)

not know good or bad persons went to Heaven or Hell or even that there were such places. He agreed with the coroner that his parents had treated him badly by not letting him go to school. The coroner stated piously that this case was one of many instances that he had found in his capacity as coroner and he said it showed 'the want of missionary and educational efforts still needed at home'.

Revill confirmed Thompson's account by saying that Ibbotson 'whizzed the stick around' at Pinder in a passion of retaliation and that it was as a response to the blow. He had met Pinder near Allen Street School and he had asked him to come with him to Acorn Street to see America. He did not tell him that he was going to strike him. The next to take the stand was Mary Ann Igge of Blue Boy Street who further shocked the assembled persons by telling them that she had not attended school since she was a small girl. She told the coroner that she had witnessed Ibbotson strike

Miss Farr the previous Monday. She had also been walking down Acorn Street on the night of the attack and had seen Ibbotson strike Pinder.

The man who had helped the boy into Ibbotson's grandmother's house was a man called William Jazer of Gibraltar Street. The boy's condition worsened and he then took him to the infirmary. He told the coroner that the unconscious boy suffered fits all the way to the hospital. Mr Hart, the hospital surgeon, stated that the deceased had been admitted at 8.10 p.m. on the Friday night. The boy was suffering from epileptic fits and was quite insensible. The wound was ¾ inch in length on his left temple and had extended through the skull and into the brain cavity. The fits continued all Friday night in rapid succession and, in consultation with other doctors, he agreed to a trepanning operation on Saturday. Trepanning operations involve opening a hole in the skull – in this case it cured the fitting, but unfortunately the boy still died. Mr Hart undertook the post-mortem and it was agreed that the injuries to the head had caused the boy's death.

William Ibbotson, who had been arrested on 16 March 1858, now took the stand and told the jury that Igge had lied and that she had been in the passage with Pinder and Thompson when Pinder hit him. He described how Pinder had rushed out of the passage and attacked him, claiming that the assault was sudden and unexpected. He could not remember hitting Pinder with the scissors and just remembered seeing the body on the floor. He also stated that he had helped to carry the body of Pinder into his grandmother's house, but this was refuted by the other witnesses. The coroner stated that although Pinder struck the first blow, Ibbotson was not justified in attacking him with the scissors and therefore he was clearly guilty of manslaughter. There were contributory factors, but that was the consideration of another tribunal.

One of the jurors, Mr William Hudson, thought that the coroner was wrong and that Ibbotson had acted clearly in self defence and therefore he ought not to go to prison. He suggested that had he been in the same position he would have done the same. The jury took a long time to decide and after two hours returned the verdict of murder by manslaughter.

Ibbotson appeared at the Assizes on 17 July 1858. No doubt the very young age of the boy counted for something as his Lordship directed the jury to return a verdict of not guilty by reason of there being very little evidence to prove that manslaughter had taken place, the second blow being given immediately after the blow by the deceased. This was not a premeditated crime and the boy had struck out in retaliation of being hit on the mouth.

Both of the last two cases happened in the heat of passion and both victims died as a result of blows, but the following case is one where long planning and preparation culminated in a brutal and premeditated murder.

Chapter Four

⋙◆⋘

The Mystery of the Watch

The weather in Sheffield in January 1847 was predictably very cold – so cold in fact that the blast furnace dam had frozen over, bringing out skaters to seize their chance while it lasted. The newspaper recorded that a game of cricket had been played on the dam by members of the Sheffield Skating Club and that 'excellent play was exhibited on both sides of the two teams'. Skating on ice was a pleasurable pastime which was an infrequent occurrence; the people of the town made the best of it while they could. The cold weather was not always as welcome, however, and on the evening of Monday 11 January a tobacconist of Waingate, Sheffield, decided that as it was so cold he would take a cab home.

Highway robbery was quite common in Victorian Sheffield. The many alleyways and back streets could provide an easy getaway for people who were familiar with the rabbit warren of the city. Many unsuspecting tradesmen carrying home their takings were attacked and robbed. This case, which took many months to solve, involved a broken watch which finally served to bring the perpetrators out into the open. It was also a prime example of the waiting game, not only for the murderers waiting for their victim, but also for the police watching suspected characters until they had enough evidence to arrest the men concerned. In researching this case, I have found many inconsistencies in its reporting – including reporters giving the main characters different addresses and different ages. For example, the home of the Palfreymans was reported as being both the Gardeners Arms on Occupation Road and Tea Garden Cottage on Grimethorpe Road. I have used my own discretion when writing up this case and so I apologize for any mistakes that have been made.

John Riley was a well-known tobacconist of the town whose routine very rarely varied. He would close up his shop and either walk home or get a cab, arriving home between 9.30 p.m. and 10 p.m., when he and his wife would have dinner and retire to bed. On Monday 11 January 1847 he varied from his routine, but it seems that someone was watching him closely. Another tradesman, William Waterman, who had a grocer's shop on the Wicker, entered Riley's tobacconist's shop about 9.15 p.m. just as he was about to lock up. Waterman bought a cigar and then they went through to the back of the shop and had a small gin and water together.

By 9.30 p.m. he had persuaded Riley to come for a quick drink with him at the New Market Inn. Riley agreed just to have one drink before going home. The two friends walked down to the inn, only stopping on the way to hire a cab from the Haymarket stand and asking the cabman to pick Riley up at 10.30 p.m. from the inn, as the cabman had done three weeks previously. The landlady of the inn, Mrs Elizabeth Tune, stated that although she had never seen Riley before, she knew Mr Waterman, who came in arm in arm with him. She said that although he was reasonably sober there was a lot of laughter and jokes coming from the table where the two men and a group of other businessmen were sitting. At half past ten the cab arrived, driven by Mr George Collis of West Street, to take Riley home – and he was asked to wait. At 11 p.m. he went inside the inn and asked his fare how much longer he would be. He was told that he would be there directly. By 11.30 p.m. the cabman was told by the landlady to go and to come back in the morning to Mr Riley's shop where he would pay him.

Eventually Riley left the pub at almost 12.30 a.m. He was described as 'being rather fresh' by the landlord of the pub – which in modern terms means tipsy rather than drunk. Whilst in the pub he had consumed several glasses of brandy and water and the matter of his sobriety would be discussed at the trial. He had started the evening joking with other tradesmen in the pub and then eventually sitting in a corner on

Above Waingate from Bridge Street junction. (Reproduced courtesy of Picture Sheffield)

Opposite The report on the inquest of John Riley. (*Sheffield & Rotherham Independent*, 16 January 1847)

RICULTURAL PRODUCE.

SHEFFIELD MARKETS.

XCHANGE, January 12.—We had a fair supply of narket this morning, and towards noon there was l of anxiety manifested among dealers as to es. Holders asked an advance of 1s. per three last week's terms, but this demand being met ct refusal on the part of the millers, business low progress for some time. Eventually the emanded being reduced to 6d., nearly all the bought up at that improvement. A few choice ld at from 9d. to 1s. more money. The sales of ter, however, were very limited. The best malt- reached 60s. per quarter, and the lowest grind- es 46s. Beans, Peas, and Oats fully maintained terms. Boiling Peas not to be had on any

red .... 23s. 0d. to 24s. 6d. per load.
ine .... 25s. 6d. to 28s. 0d. —
hite .... 26s. 6d. to 27s. 6d. —
ine .... 28s. 6d. to 30s. 0d. —
(malting) .... 46s. 0d. to 60s. 0d. per qr.
grinding) .... 46s. 0d. to 48s. 0d. —
.... 20s. 0d. to 21s. 6d. —
.... 19s. 6d. to 20s. 0d. —
.... 26s. 0d. to 35s. 0d. —

's WEEKLY CORN RETURN.—An account of the ies and Prices of British Corn sold in Sheffield Market returns delivered to the Inspector by the Dealers, in k ending Tuesday, Jan. 12, 1847, computed by the d Imperial Measure of 8 Gallons to the Bushel.

	Imp. Measure. Total Quant.		Total Amount.			Price per Qr. Imp. Measure.		
	Qrs.	Bls.	£.	s.	d.	£.	s.	d.
....	199	4	699	1	7	3	10	1
....	190	0	500	6	8	2	12	8
....	102	0	142	7	6	1	7	11
....	0	0	0	0	0	0	0	0
....	3	6	10	10	0	2	16	0
....	1	4	4	2	0	2	14	8

BREAD IN SHEFFIELD.—Best household bread, 8d. per nds do., 7d.; Brown do., 6d.

ARKET, Jan. 12.—The market was moderately vith Fodder. Prices of all articles about the same ek.

.... 60s. to 85s. per ton.
Straw.............. 30s. to 34s. —
t Straw .... 28s. to 31s. —
ips, (white & yellow) 15s. to 16s. —
e .... 21s. to 23s. —

AND PIG MARKET, Jan. 12.—There was a nu- ow of Beasts at market, and many exchanged last week's figures. Pigs were less plentiful. to 7s. 6d. per stone.

TILLAGES.

XCHANGE, January 12.—A few orders for Guano tillages for future delivery. Salt scarce and in and. Prices as last quoted.

Peruvian,) .. £10. 0s. per ton, or 10s. 6d. per cwt
chaboe,) .. £8. 10s. „ or 9s. 0d. „
Patagonian,) £7. 10s. „ or 8s. 0d. „
Possession Island,) £6. „ or 6s. 6d. „
Sahdanha Bay) £7. 0s. „ or 7s. 6d. „
tural Salt.................. 20s. 0d. per ton.
do. soiled .... 21s. 0d. „
lt, in squares .... 30s. 0d. „
n, do. .... 26s. 0d. „
n, stoved .... 28s. 0d. „
ke, for Cattle .... 18s. 6d. „
n, Sulphate of Lime .... 28s. 0d. „
of Soda .... 19s. 6d. per cwt.
of Potass, Saltpetre .... 33s. 6d. „
te of Amonia .... 21s. 6d. „
ed Charcoal (for mixing with Guano, &c.,) 5s.
shes .... 7s. 0d. per quarter.
harcoal .... 7s. 0d. „
on's, English Guano .... £5. 0s. per ton.
Compost .... £3. 0s. „
.... £6. 10s. to £7. 0s. „
ced Bones .... £6. 0s. „
d Cake, English .. £8. 0s. to £10. 10s. „
Foreign...... £8. 0s. to £9. 0s. „

ONDON AND COUNTRY MARKETS.

N CORN EXCHANGE, MONDAY, Jan. 11.—There r supply of Wheat and Spring Corn fresh up to his morning, and the trade opened with a cautious- he part of the buyers generally. On the whole, t trade has been quiet, at the prices of this day d for Barley about 2s. advanced rates have been ats have found buyers at 6d. to 1s. over Friday's ut the extent of business done has not been large, e 2s. dearer. The high rates paid for Peas of all e checked purchases, and, to make sales, nothing day's advance was obtainable. In Flour or Malt o change in value. Seeds are all firm in regard tions, without much activity in purchases.

N, Wednesday.—We had an unusually short sup- nglish Wheat on show to-day. Although the at- of buyers was small, the demand was steady, at ut at nothing quotable beyond) Monday's prices, hich most of the samples were disposed of. There od inquiry for fine Foreign Wheat, at extreme es. Inferior bonded Wheats were held at 1s. per more money. In the value of the best descrip- variation was noticed. The demand for Barley

SECOND EDITION.

INDEPENDENT OFFICE, Saturday Night, Quarter-past Nine o'Clock.

DEATH OF MR. JOHN RILEY.

INQUEST ON THE BODY.

The town, this morning, was shocked by the report that Mr. John Riley, upon whom a robbery, with great violence, was committed, on Monday night, (of which an account appears in our last page,) had died during the night. Throughout yesterday he had been delirious, and during the evening, he was considered to be in great danger. He expired shortly before two o'clock this morning.

At half-past six in the evening, the Coroner met a most respectable Jury, at the house of the deceased, to commence his inquisition on the body. The gentlemen summoned on the inquest were, Ald. Lowe, foreman; Ald. J. Hall, Councillors Michael Hunter, R. Marsden, J. S. Nanson, H. D. Wilkinson, Messrs. C. Hawksworth, W. Ragg, Jenkinson, Broadbent, Geo. Wall, Geo. Walker, W. Lockwood, and George Bassett.

The CORONER explained to the Jury, that he would not have summoned them at so late an hour on the Saturday night, but that the policeman informed him that the family of the deceased wished to inter the body as early as possible. On the first occasion, when the policeman came to him, he did not possess all the information that he (the Coroner) thought necessary, nor was that supplied till two o'clock this afternoon, when he issued his summons for the Jury to meet from half-past six to a quarter to seven. They would now open the inquiry, but there was no probability that it could be finished to-night. It would be necessary to adjourn to another day, for it was most important that a full and proper inquiry should be made. As he observed that several members of the Town Council were present, he reminded them that they were exempt. [Alderman Lowe said they were aware of that, but they attended voluntarily.] He was very glad that they should do so, as the case was one of considerable importance.

The Jury were then sworn, and the Coroner briefly stated the facts:—On Monday, Mr. Riley was attending to his business as usual, and at night was at the New Market Inn. He left the house at a late hour to go home, and on the way was robbed and ill-used. Mr. Jackson, the surgeon, was sent for the next morning, and attended the deceased till he died. It would be a very painful circumstance if it should appear that death was caused by the violence of the men who robbed and ill-used him.

Elizabeth Tune, wife of James Tune, of the New Market Inn, Cattle market: I never saw Mr. John Riley before last Monday night, when he was in the bar of our public-house. I first saw him there about a quarter to eleven. Mr. W. Waterman, grocer, Wicker, came in with Mr. Riley, and went with him to order a cab. The deceased and Mr. Waterman sat together, joking. I saw Mr. Riley again soon after eleven. Some of the gentlemen present, with whom Mr. Riley and Mr. Waterman were joking, wished them to retire, but Mr. Waterman was unwilling, and Mr. Riley changed his seat. About half-past eleven, Mr. Riley asked me to desire the cabman, who was waiting for him, to go, and call the next day to be paid. The man had been waiting from half-past ten. I told the man to go. It was then about a quarter to twelve. Mr. Riley sat a short time longer, and then went away. It was from twelve to half-past when Mr. Riley left our house. He went out alone. Mr. Waterman and others remained in the bar. Mr. Riley had three glasses of spirits at our house, but I cannot say of what, because I did not serve him. Mr. Riley appeared quite comfortable and cheerful when he left, and walked steadily down the passage, having bid me good night. I would not say that he was not tipsy, or under the influence of liquor. I did not perceive that he was fresh at the time, but I was told so after. I did not see a drunken man in the bar. He was not drunk. I will not swear that he was not. He might be a little elevated, but I believe he was not tipsy. My husband filled Mr. Riley what he had to drink. No unpleasant words passed in the room, in my presence. There were no strangers in the bar. They were gentlemen who frequently come to the house, and I know all of them by sight.... By the Jury: I have not said that Mr. Riley left in company with Mr. Waterman. Mr. Riley assigned no reason for sending away the cab.

George Collis, of West street, cab proprietor, No. 7: Mr. Riley and a gentleman came to me on Monday evening, a few minutes before ten, on the Haymarket stand, and desired me to be at the New Market Inn at half-past ten. I went at the time exactly, and waited an hour and a quarter, when the landlady told me I might go, and call in the morning on Mr. Riley to be paid. It was just a quarter to twelve as I passed the Town Hall, after leaving the Inn. Have not seen Mr. Riley since. When Mr. Riley came to me, he came up Waingate, and appeared quite sober.... ordered. I found no other money about him but the 25s. He did not see which way the men went, nor did he say that he saw any watchman. It was Mr. Riley's practice to dine at the shop.

Cranfield Baguley, watchman, of Gibraltar street, said, I have been a watchman since the 19th August. I was on duty at half-past eight last night. My beat is from the Station Inn, Wicker, to the tea gardens on Grimesthorpe road, and back to the Station Inn. That is the first half-hour. The second beat is half way up the right of the Wicker, and then turning to the left up to Willey street end. I go down Sheldon row back again to the far end of Willey street, and round by the Tower Wheel to Blonk street, and then down the Wicker to the Station Inn at the end of the hour. My beat from half-past eleven to twelve, is up the Wicker, as I have stated, for the second half-hour. From twelve to half-past, from the Station Inn up the Occupation road; and, from half-past twelve to one, up the Wicker again. During Monday night, I regularly went my beats. I did not know Mr. Riley. I heard no disturbance. I did not see three persons together. I have not had it pointed out to me where there was a pool of blood where Mr. Riley was knocked down. The fact of the robbery has been named. I never heard exactly where it was done. I had my light that night. I was sober. I never take any liquor. I was up and down this this road every hour during the night. I did not see any man lay on the road. I was not in Palfreyman's or any other public-house that night, except at the Bull and Oak, where I had a glass of ale from 10 to 11. Now I recollect I had not any ale. I called there to know at what hour the master required to be called up. I had no drink that night at all. Don't know Palfreyman's son. Had no conversation with any railway man. Had a conversation with two men, one of whom appeared tipsy, as they were going to Grimesthorpe, about the middle of the night at the top of Spital hill. They did not say where they were going. A third man did not come up while I was with them. I did not know them. They went on towards Grimesthorpe. I believe it was between twelve and one o'clock. One was dressed in dark coat and trousers. The other had on a fustian coat with short laps. Don't know what a shooting-jacket is. Know what a shooting-coat is, but there are so many names for them. The conversation was opposite the shop of Green, the grocer. Neither of the men had any stick or weapon that I saw. I cannot tell what they said. When they left me they bid me good night.

By the Jury: I saw one man, at half-past eleven, near the railway station. He was going towards Grimesthorpe. Have never been examined as a witness.... By Mr. Hunter, in order to correct an error of the witness: Came on my beat at half-past eight. I stop in the Wicker the first half-hour. My first round is up the Occupation road, from nine to half-past.... By Ald. Lowe: I have been only nine or ten nights on the beat. I know the place where the robbery took place.... [Ald. Hall remarked, that the watchman would be going up the Wicker when Mr. Riley set off to go home, so that they would be going in opposite directions.] I first heard of the robbery from the milkman, on Wednesday night, about nine o'clock. I heard again from a gentleman. I was told of it by one of the sergeants on duty, on Wednesday night, about 12. I have been examined by Mr. Raynor about it. That was on Wednesday night; it was Thursday night before I came on duty. .. [The Coroner remarked, that if the witness did his duty, he must have passed the place of the robbery from one to half-past one.].... Witness: I go up Tom-Cross lane, but not every hour, only sometimes in the night. I was in it twice that night. Once was with the milkman, when he wet home. The other time was after two o'clock.... Mr. Hunter remarked, that the watchman's duty was to go as far as the Circus, near to the public-house whence Mr. Riley came, as well as past the spot where the robbery took place....... Mr. Riley remarked, that his brother must have lain some time on the spot where he was knocked down.... Witness: I met the night-sergeant that night, at twenty-five minutes past eleven, in the Wicker. There was no person I knew in the Bull and Oak.

The Coroner suggested the adjournment of the inquest, for the purpose of further inquiry. After some conversation, the Coroner named Thursday afternoon, at the Hall Carr Hotel, for the time and place of adjournment.

Before adjourning, the Coroner and Jury proceeded to view the body. The face presented a shocking spectacle. It was so much disfigured that gentlemen who had known the deceased well, declared they should have been unable to recognize him. Very severe blows had been inflicted on the forehead, over each eye, and upon the nose. The upper part of the face was one mass of blackness. Upon both knees there was extensive abrasion of the skin, as though from a violent struggle upon the ground, from which it seems not improbable that the deceased, who was a stout, muscular man, made more resistance than he was himself aware of.

The rumour is current in the town that Arthur Palfreyman, of Occupation road, and John Jones, of Townhead st., are in custody, charged with this grave offence. The fact is not so. The charge against them is that of stealing from a railway carriage, on Friday night, a sack of leather, on which charge they have been examined before the Mayor, and remanded to Tuesday.

SPORTING INTELLIGENCE.

HUNTING APPOINTMENTS.

his own sipping at the spirits that had been served to him. The landlord of the pub served his drinks, but could not remember how many he had consumed. Most of his customers were regulars, there were no suspicious characters and there had been no quarrelling or dissention whilst Riley had been there. However, there was some dissent later as to what time Riley had left that night. The landlord's wife said that he left at 12.30 a.m., leaving Mr Waterman in the bar. Riley corroborated this when he told his wife that he had left on his own, leaving Mr Waterman in the public house. Mr Waterman, however, remembered leaving before 11.30 p.m. as the cab was still waiting. He had urged his friend to take the cab and go home, but instead Riley told him that he had made the decision to walk home and sent the cab away. Waterman certainly thought Riley was capable of walking home by himself.

Riley proceeded to go home, and he later told his wife that he was passing a house on Occupation Road he heard some men say, 'Damn, he's here!' He was then hit on the forehead with a blunt instrument and fell to the ground. When he came round a short while later, he managed to drag himself to his feet. There was blood everywhere, and as he leaned against a wall to get his breath, he left bloodstains on the wall. He clutched hold of a garden gate and noticed that he had left blood on it as he slowly made his way home (which was a few yards up the road). Later the people in the house outside of which he was attacked stated that they had heard no disturbance that night and knew nothing about the attack until the police constable called the following morning. Despite the fact that the owner of the house, one Elizabeth Taylor,

Haymarket as it looks today. (Chris Drinkall)

had reported that she did not go to bed until midnight and was up two or three times during the night as she was drying clothes in front of the fire, she still had heard nothing which caused her any concern. She pointed out that they had a dog that barked at the slightest noise but even he had not barked that evening.

Therefore, when her husband arrived home at 1.40 a.m. on the Tuesday morning in a dreadful state, Mrs Riley was shocked and surprised. His face was bruised and battered and covered in dirt, and his braces were broken. There was evidence that there had been a struggle, his trousers were torn at the knees and he had two black eyes. Riley told her that he had been hit over the head and she saw that he had a large lump on his head, which was bleeding badly. His nose was covered in blood and his bruised hands also had blood on them. Riley said that he had lost his hat and his stick and the right-hand pocket of his trousers had been pulled inside out. He had about 30s in that pocket (although there was silver amounting to 25s in the other pocket, which was untouched). He also found his watch was missing. Riley remembered that three men had attacked him as he approached Tom Cross Lane. He did not know any of the men, although he was sure, judging by one of the men's speech, that at least one was from Grimethorpe. They struck at him and he fell to the ground unconscious. When he awoke he found himself in a pool of blood and the men had gone. He told his wife, 'Mary, they have nearly killed me'. His wife bathed his head and wanted to call for the doctor, but Riley insisted that he just wanted to have a good night's sleep and they both retired to bed. He slept very badly and complained of pains where he had been struck in the head. In the morning, despite his protestations, Dr Henry Jackson was called. The doctor arrived at 9 a.m. on the Tuesday morning, and administered to him as best as he could for the rest of the week, but his condition gradually deteriorated, and Riley died at 2 a.m. on Saturday 16 January. For the most part he was delirious and sliding in and out of consciousness and the doctor testified that whilst he could still speak, he had told him that he had no knowledge of the identity of the three men.

The inquest was called for Tuesday evening, 19 January, at the unusual hour of 6.30 p.m., and was held at the house of the deceased man. The coroner apologized for the lateness of the hour, but told the jury that he had been waiting for certain information, which he had only received at 2 p.m. that day. It was later determined that the information concerned some men who had been brought into custody. Although questioned by the magistrate, Mr Overend, all had been released and no charges had been made against them. He told the jury that due to the lateness of the hour that he would just hear the depositions and the medical evidence and then adjourned the inquest for a further period of time. Mrs Riley gave her deposition first. She stated that when her husband had left that morning, about 9 a.m., he was in his usual good spirits and health. He had not returned for his evening meal as expected.

A nightwatchman was then called, who gave his name as Cranfield Baguley of Gibraltar Street. This man gave so many conflicting statements that it is difficult to put any credence on any of his evidence which was to become crucial to the case. He began by stating that his beat was from the Station Hotel on the Wicker to the

The Station Hotel, the Wicker. (Chris Drinkall)

Spital Hill in 1900. (Reproduced courtesy of Picture Sheffield)

tea gardens on Grimesthorpe Road and, with some diversions, ended back at the Station Hotel. He told the inquest that he did not know Riley personally and that he covered his beat every hour throughout the night. He stated that the night had been quiet, only disturbed by a conversation with two unknown men at the top of Spital Hill outside a greengrocers between midnight and 1 a.m., one of whom he described as tipsy.

A third man joined them and when they left they walked towards the Grimethorpe Road. He stated that none of the men had a stick or a weapon that he saw. He then went on to contradict himself again by telling the jury and the coroner that he had not had any ale at all that night and then later said that he had a glass of ale at the Bull and Oak on the Wicker. Then he recollected that he hadn't had any ale at all, but had called in to ask the master of the Bull and Oak what time he wanted waking up. A member of the jury reckoned that by his beat he should have been near to the scene of the robbery about 1.30 a.m., but Baguley reiterated that he had been in the area and had seen no body and no disturbances. Riley's brother, who attended the inquest, pointed out to the watchman that due to the severity of the wounds inflicted on his brother that he must have lain on the ground for some time before recovering and going home and therefore he should have been seen earlier. Baguley said that he 'goes up Occupation Road, but not every hour, but at some point every night'. He completed his evidence by stating that he had heard of the robbery on Wednesday night from a milkman he had met on his rounds. At this point it was almost 9.30 p.m. and the coroner adjourned the inquest to be held at the Hall Carr Hotel the following Thursday, 21 January. But before the jury left, they were asked to look at the body of the deceased man. It was reported that he was so disfigured that he would not have been recognisable. It was obvious that even a week following the attack that he had been the victim of a very violent struggle.

At the adjourned inquest it seems that the watch belonging to Riley had been found under somewhat curious circumstances. The watch was produced by William Hudson of 3 Bright Lane, the Wicker, who said that he had made the coffin for Riley and that when he went to fetch the coffin board from his house, he had found the watch wrapped up in a black cloth with pins in, making it look like a ball. It was laid about five or six yards from the front entrance gates within the garden of the property of the deceased man. The watch was shown to the jury and it was noted that the glass was broken, the swivel was lost and the figures on the watch face were broken. Hudson gave the watch to a member of the deceased man's family and then later, realizing it would be needed as evidence, took the watch to the Town Hall and gave it to Superintendent Raynor. Aldermen Lowe on the bench stated that he had visited the house on Sunday and stated categorically that if the watch had lain there he would have seen it.

The next person was Henry Jackson, the surgeon, who described Riley's injuries when he visited him on the Tuesday morning. He noted that there were no wounds or swelling at the back of the head, proving that he had been attacked from the front. Riley, who was still conscious and lucid at that point, told him that he felt the blow to his forehead and he remembered no more until he regained consciousness. He told the surgeon that he had no idea how long he had been unconscious. At that time, Riley didn't complain of any pain but rather a 'stiffness in his head' and he told the surgeon that during the previous evening he had bled from the nose. Despite minimizing his wounds, Jackson recognised that he was in grave danger and said as much to Riley. The surgeon asked him if he minded getting a second opinion and when Riley agreed, Jackson called in Dr Bartelome, who concurred with his diagnosis. The poor man rapidly began to deteriorate over the next few days and by Thursday 14 January he was delirious. Jackson told the jury that by Friday his patient was described as 'wild and rambling'. After his death on the Saturday, Dr Jackson completed the post-mortem and he reported that he found that the body of the deceased man to be stout and well formed. Death was caused by a violent blow to the head inflicted by a blunt instrument occasioning loss of blood and causing shock to the nervous system that triggered delirium tremens. The magistrate questioned him on this matter, as it was usually overindulgence in alcoholic liquor which caused delirium tremens, but Dr Jackson assured him that it was due to shock and stated he had known of other cases where this had happened. The question had been brought up about the quantity of liquor that Riley had taken and as to his suitability to get home safely. Dr Jackson was asked by a member of the jury if falling down whilst intoxicated could cause such injuries and he replied, with some authority, 'certainly not'.

During the police investigation some suspicion had been cast on Mr Anthony Palfreyman, a mason. He told the jury that he lived with his mother and father at Tea Garden Cottage on the Grimesthorpe Road. On the night of Monday 11 January he was at the Old White Lion on the Wicker from 9.30 p.m. to 6.30 a.m. the following day. He had too much to drink and asked the landlord if there was somewhere he could stay. He did not sleep in a bed, but on a form in the back room. He told the coroner that he had been drinking with a young man named Henry Earnshaw, who was with him until about 11 p.m. that night. There were other people in the house, but they couldn't say with any certainty what time he retired to the back room. He stated that he frequently went to the Old White Lion and stayed the night, and he offered the explanation that he had been in trouble with his father due to being in custody for stealing some leather with another young man, called John Jones, and thought it might be better to stay out of sight. He was on friendly terms with the landlord of the public house, who had lent him some blankets to sleep on. The landlord agreed that Palfreyman had stayed all night and he returned home the following morning at some time between 6 a.m. and 7 a.m. It was when he returned home that his mother told him that there had been a robbery in the early hours of Tuesday 12 January. His father next took the stand and he explained that he had also first heard about the robbery on Tuesday when it had been discussed with his wife and son, Anthony. He said that the previous evening he had arrived home at 11 p.m. His son, George, came in at the same time and he asked him to stay up as Anthony was still out and to let him in, which George agreed to do. He and his wife then went to bed. George corroborated his father's evidence, stating that he had waited for Anthony until about 1 a.m. when he went to bed. He also had heard about the robbery from his mother. The next person to take the stand was his mother, Mrs Jane Palfreyman, who contradicted herself with

Snow Lane looking downwards. (Chris Drinkall)

Snow Lane looking upwards. (Chris Drinkall)

her evidence. She at first stated that when she had gone to bed with her husband at about 11.30 p.m. that no one had stayed up to wait for Anthony's return. She then recollected that George had stayed downstairs to wait up. These contradictions must have confused the jury and the coroner when summing up the evidence. At that point the only verdict which the jury was able to bring in was one of 'willful murder by person or persons unknown'.

Some men named by Anthony Palfreyman as being in the bar of the Old White Lion had been taken into custody and questioned, but released. It seems that the chief constable had received some important information which had brought suspicion on the men and a careful watch had been on two of the men, named as Challenor and Bradley. As a result of this, further evidence had been obtained and the two men were apprehended. It was not until April that rumours were spreading through the city that three men had been arrested on suspicion of highway robbery. Inspector Astwood arrested James Bradley, aged twenty-three, on Friday 9 April at a house in Snow Lane about 11 p.m., and he was brought to the Town Hall.

William Challenor had been arrested an hour earlier. After listening to the statement made by James Bradley which implicated his brother George, aged twenty-six, he also was arrested on the 11 April. These three men appeared before the two magistrates, Mr Wilson Overend and the Mayor on Thursday 14 April 1847. The story had produced such interest that it was reported that the courtroom was crowded with people wanting to see the prisoners. The charge was that on the early hours of 12 January they 'with malice aforethought killed and murdered John Riley and also with having violently robbed him of his silver watch and 30s in silver'. It seems that Challenor had been in the Old White Lion on the evening of 11 January and upon leaving had asked the innkeeper for the loan of a scarf as he had been ill and the night was cold. It was thought that he wanted a scarf to avoid identification in carrying out the robbery. His mother returned the scarf the next day. He agreed that he had left the pub with James Bradley about 11.45 p.m. on the night of the robbery and had spoken to the watchman on the way. Then he and James had parted company, both going to their separate homes.

The nightwatchman, Baguley, once again contradicted his previous statement where he had said that he did not know the men he had spoken to by stating that 'he knew the men and they were the prisoners'.

One of the prosecution witnesses, George Bowling, who knew both the brothers, stated that he lodged at the Coach and Horses in Water Lane. He had seen George Bradley on Thursday 14 January and he had called to him to come outside the public house and they walked to West Bar. During the walk, Bradley asked him to pawn a watch for him and showed him the watch which was without glass or a swivel. Bowling suggested that they take it to a man called George Sales who would buy it and they proceeded to his workshop. Bowling now called to Sales to come outside and he showed him the watch. Sales had no money with him, but borrowed the money from an acquaintance and later gave Bowling 17s for the watch. Bowling gave Bradley 15s of the money and they went to the All Nations pub for a drink. In this place, and with quite a few drinks in him, Bradley told the other two men that 'you must say nothing about the watch as it came from Mr Riley, the tobacconist on Waingate'. He

Angel Street as it looks today. (Chris Drinkall)

went on to describe how 'I robbed him of his watch and 30s. I knocked him down with the first blow… I stood at the top of lane near to the tea garden and waited for him coming'. On Sunday 17 January, following the death of Riley the previous evening, Bowling described how he had met George Bradley, who told him that he had heard that Riley was dead. He then contradicted himself, stating that 'it was a bad job. It was not me that gave him the blow, it was someone else but I will stick staunch if I get hung for it'. Bowling told him that he had seen Sales, who told him that after hearing of the robbery he had realized that the watch in his possession had belonged to the dead man and he was determined to be rid of it. He had cut some cloth from a dark coat (which he described as blue) and the following day Sunday, the 17th, had placed it on the footpath of Mr Riley's garden. Following the finding of the watch and the confession of James Bradley, Inspector Astwood went to Sales' workshop and was shown the remnants of the coat in which the watch had been wrapped in, resulting in the arrest of George Bradley.

The two brothers were examined. James Bradley agreed that it was himself and William Challenor who had a conversation with the watchman at the top of Spital Hill that night before going home. He said that after about half an hour his brother, George, arrived back at the house and had showed him the watch.

George's statement said that he had left a public house in Angel Street at 1 a.m. and walked up Occupation Road, where he found Riley very drunk and leaning against a wall with blood pouring from his head. The watch and some silver were lying strewn about in the road. George said that he had tried to lift him up and told him that he had found the money in the road but Riley rejected his help and told him, 'Damn you go. I can do without you'. When the prosecution challenged him that the statement he had made to Bowling and Sales was that he had knocked Riley to the floor, George denied it saying that 'I'll take my oath that I didn't say that'. He then said that Riley had told him that he had fallen down about three times on his way home. George left him and went home and gave his brother the watch. At this point, Mr Overend consulted with the Mayor and they both agreed that much evidence was still being sought and they would adjourn the enquiry to a later date, which would be arranged once the evidence had all been gathered in. The adjourned proceedings met on Saturday 17 April at the Town Hall, but given the seriousness of the crimes facing them it appeared that it was swiftly adjourned once more to Monday 19 April in order that the prisoners could get legal advice.

At the hearing in front of Mr Wilson Overend, it seems that William Challoner had been released as the evidence against him was slim, apart from the fact that he had been seen in the company of James Bradley on the night of the robbery. The witnesses statements had been taken and the two brothers appeared in the dock for sentencing. It was reported that James appeared cheerful and in good spirits. His brother, however, looked pale and nervous and his head was 'hung down' as the statements were read out. The clerk read out the charge of 'highway robbery with violence and murder' and both men pleaded not guilty. George Bradley stated that he had been drinking in a lot of pubs that night and could not be sure of what time he had left for home. However, for the most part this was all the evidence he could produce. The prisoners were asked if they agreed with the statements made by the witnesses and James stated that some of the witnesses were not telling the truth. George asked that when Riley had told him that he had fallen three times that this information be included in his statement and this change was added.

The jury, after a short consultation, agreed that both men were guilty of the crime and that they be sentenced to trial at the next York Assizes. James' demeanour did not change when the verdict had been delivered but when an unknown woman was heard to sob loudly in the court, George appeared to be particularly distressed. The trial was held on 24 July 1847 when once again both brothers pleaded 'not guilty'.

However the evidence against them was too strong. In his summing up, the judge stated that it was a proven fact that both brothers were out at the time the robbery was committed and that they had both handled the stolen watch. Nevertheless, the case had shown that the robbery had been planned and they were waiting for Riley as he made his way home. By their actions, malice aforethought had clearly been shown and the jury acknowledged this was a premeditated act of murder and not a crime of manslaughter. The jury returned after half an hour and pronounced the men guilty of murder. The judge said that in view of the seriousness of the crime that both men be sentenced to transportation for fifteen years. The arrogance of James Bradley showed through when he stated 'that's nowt' as they took him back to the cells.

Transportation for fifteen years was a hard sentence to be handed out, but there were some things to look forward to. A prisoner could apply for a ticket of leave after

GEORGE BRADLEY.   JAMES BRADLEY.

TRIAL OF GEORGE AND JAMES BRADLEY
FOR THE
MURDER OF MR. RILEY, AT SHEFFIELD.

YORKSHIRE ASSIZES.
[Continued from the Supplement.]

CROWN COURT.

WEDNESDAY.—Before Mr. Justice WIGHTMAN.

GEORGE BRADLEY, 26, and JAMES BRADLEY, 23, were charged with the wilful murder of John Riley, at Sheffield, on the 12th of January last.

COUNSEL.—For the prosecution; Mr. Sergeant WILKINS, Mr. PICKERING, and Mr. PEARCE. For the prisoner George Bradley, Mr. MATTHEWS; and for James Bradley, Mr. OVEREND.

ATTORNEYS.—For the prosecution, Mr. Eyre, of Sheffield; and for the prisoners, Mr. Dale, of York.

The prisoners pleaded Not Guilty.

The counsel for the prisoner, as the names of the jury-men were called over, objected to all who resided in or came from the neighbourhood of Sheffield. When the Jury had been properly empanelled,

Mr. Wilkins stated the case. He said,—May it please your Lordship and the gentlemen of the Jury; the two young men now standing in the dock are indicted for the wilful murder of Mr. John Riley. My duty to-day is a very simple and straightforward one. I have merely to lay before you the facts out of which this occurrence arises. Having done so, and called the evidence before you to substantiate these facts, my duty will be done. Mr. John Riley, the deceased, was a man about 44 years of age, carrying on business as a tobacconist, in Waingate, in Sheffield. His place of residence was at Broom-leys, about a mile from Sheffield, on the road to Grimesthorpe. You will see, by the plan which I now hand to you, that his residence was a little to the west of the lane or road. It appears that, on the night of Monday, the 11th of January last, he closed his shop in Waingate about nine o'clock. The shutters were put to, but the door left open, and a gentleman named Waterman, who was passing, being an acquaintance of his, and seeing the door open, went in to inquire how he was. Mr. Riley requested him to walk into a little back room, and there they together had one glass of gin and water. At half-past nine, he left his shop in company with Mr. Waterman, and went to an inn in Sheffield, called the New Cattle Market Inn. On their road there they passed by the cabstand in front of the Tontine, and there Mr. Riley directed a cabman named Collis to be at the Cattle Market Inn, with his cab, at half-past ten o'clock, to take him home, it being his usual custom to go home in a cab. They went from there to the inn, where they met with several other gentlemen who were regaling themselves, like Mr. Riley and Mr. Waterman sat down, and indulged in conversation, and it was remarked that he appeared very jocular and in very high spirits. It will be proved that he drank, in the course of the evening, about three sixpenny glasses of brandy and water. At half-past ten o'clock the cab came, as ordered, and the driver will tell you that when he left the cab-stand he looked at the Town-Hall clock, and that it was half-past to a minute; that when he got to the public-house, which is very near, he went into the passage to look at the clock, and discovered that it was a quarter of an hour later than he remember. The landlady of the inn was that night at the

obtained change, gave her three shillings back. Bowling and Bradley went back together to the Coach and Horses. In about an hour, according to the request of Sayles, Bowling went out to see if he had got the money. Whilst he was gone James Bradley asked the landlord to let him have some ale, stating that he should have some money when Bowling came back, and in consequence of this, I believe the landlord let him have two quarts of ale. He asked the landlord if he had heard of Mr. Riley's robbery. This you will remember was on Thursday night. The landlord replied no, he had not. Upon which Bradley remarked that they must be very queer sort of thieves who laid done it, for they had left 'three quid,' (meaning £3,) and the shop keys in one of his pockets. It is rather important that you should remember this fact. Bowling, whilst they were in conversation, came back, stating he could not find Sayles, and he should have to go again for the money. They sat together a short time, when Sayles came in, and beckoned Bowling into the street, and there paid him 17s. for the watch. Bowling came in and gave Bradley 13s., keeping 12s. for himself. The landlord will tell you, that almost immediately after this, Bradley gave him a half-crown in payment for the ale he had had before, and received change out of it. After they had been sitting together some time, they all three, (Sayles, James Bradley, and Bowling,) went to the All Nations, another public-house in the same street. They there continued drinking together, and perhaps that may have thrown James Bradley off his guard; but whether that be so or not, if you believe Bowling and Sayles,—and it appears to me there are many circumstances which tend to corroborate their story,—the prisoner Bradley then made this statement to them,—"You must say nothing about the watch; it came from Mr. Riley, the tobacconist, of Waingate. I robbed him of his watch and thirty shillings. I knocked him down the first blow. I have heard that I missed three pounds, and the shop-door keys. I have heard that Mr. Riley got home between two and three o'clock in the morning. He was by himself." The medical men will tell you that such a blow as caused Mr. Riley's death would knock him down. If this statement which I have read be true—and I know of no evidence against a man so strong as that which he volunteers, and which comes from his own mouth—if it be true that he robbed him,—if it be true that he knocked him down by the first blow,—if it be true that he is afterwards found in possession of property that was stolen from the murdered man, it is for you to say to what conclusion these facts lead. It will be shewn, that upon that same evening (Monday, the 11th) when Mr. Riley was attacked, James Bradley, in company with a named Chaliner, came to Sheffield at seven o'clock. They are seen together at the White Lion. The White Lion, Gentlemen, is at the top of the Wicker, and facing the street in which the New Cattle Market Hotel, where Mr. Riley was spending the evening, is situated. Whilst they were at the White Lion, the landlord will tell you that Bradley kept going to the door, and looking out, and then came back again into the house. The gas lamps were lighted; and I believe a person standing at the door of the White Lion could see a great way down the street. One thing is quite clear, viz, he was constantly going out, as if looking for somebody, and this upon the night and shortly before the hour when Mr. Riley was attacked. They leave there, and are next seen together by a watchman near Mr. Green's

Wm. Waterman examined by Mr. Pearce: A residing in the Wicker, in Sheffield. Remember the 11th July. Saw the late Mr. Riley at b Waingate, at about a quarter-past nine at night me to go in, and I did so. We had a little gi together—not as much as is generally sold a threepence each.... [Mr. Wilkins: The Jury stand that better than your Lordship. (Lang We remained there about a quarter of an ho about half-past nine. Mr. Riley went with n gate to the cab stand, opposite the Tontine Ho Mr. Riley give directions there to a cabman to Cattle Market Inn at half-past ten o'clock. M man perfectly sober to the best of my opinion. from the cab-stand to Mr. Tune's, the New Ca Inn. I remained there till half-past eleven, to twelve. There were several other parties was Mr. Harrison, the architect. I left Mr. bar. He was very cheerful and jocular—no He had been drinking, but I did not notice wh I have not seen him since. The cabman ca waiting an hour.... Cross-examined by Mr. Had been a friend of Mr. Riley, and had kn or 15 years. He had not been in the habit Tune's of an evening, or at any other inn that of. I had not been with him of a long time met him then purely accidental. I can't tell had been taking any wine or spirits during t was very lively, but did not appear to have t Besides Mr. Harrison, there were eight or te Tune's. Did not see any railway labourers not hear Mr. Riley make my boasting abou don't know that there were other persons in besides those in the bar. I know a man n who is a grocer. Don't know Geo. Bowling.

Geo. Collis, examined by Mr. Serjeant Wilk last, was driving a cab for my brother Pete nine and ten, on Jan. 11th, was opposite the T Mr. Riley came with Mr. Waterman, and ga to call at the New Cattle Market Inn at h Went there at that time precisely by the Town The distance is very short. On getting ther the passage and saw Mr. Riley, and by hi waited. When in the passage, noticed the was a quarter-past ten. After waiting som Tune desired me to go home. In order to fare, went to look at the clock, and it was l Went directly to the Town-Hall, and that it ter to twelve. Saw Mr. Riley several times, th a quarter of an hour before leaving, he th sober.... Cross-examined by Mr. Matthews taken Mr. Riley home once before. Saw oth Tune's: they all appeared respectable. Th railway labourers that I saw.

Elizabeth Tune, examined by Mr. Pickeri band, James Tune, keeps the New Cattle Mar member the night of Monday, the 11th Jan. Circus, which is next door but one to our h there about a quarter to eleven, and noticed a at the door. There were many persons in t among them Mr. Riley, but there was none room. Afterwards sent the cab away. Mr. little after twelve. He was then not perfectly toxicated—a little elevated.... Cross-examin Overend: Did not see the cabman come in Riley to go home.... Re-examined: Cann clearly out of the bar into the tap-room.... I ship: Some persons came in the tap room aft did not see any of them. When the cabman there was no one in the tap-room—they had al

James Tune, examined by Mr. Pearce: Ke Cattle Market Inn. Remember Monday, the 1 Mr. Riley came to my house that night, abou nine, in company with Mr. Waterman. He sa against the window near the street. Mr. Har fect, was there, and some others. I waited upo He had, to the best of my belief, three 6d. brandy and water. Remember a cab coming and the man coming in to ask for Mr. Riley said he was not quite ready—he must wait a Riley left near 12 o'clock—a little before or r He was perfectly capable of walking home, care of himself. He walked perfectly stead examined by Mr. Overend: Did not notice M go away. Don't know the exact time Mr. R cept that it was about 12 o'clock.

Mrs. Tune recalled, and examined by Mr. C was a quarter of an hour after Mr. Harrison that Mr. Riley left.

James Harrison, examined by Mr. Pickeri architect, residing at Sheffield. Remember 11th January, was at the New Market Inn, a Riley there. Left at five minutes to twelve, Riley sober. He was sober, sufficiently, to wal take care of himself when I left.... Cross-e Mr. Matthews: It was a fine night—not fros It was wintery weather, but fine for the even know that there was snow outside the town Overend: I looked at the clock in the bar as to see that I could get home by twelve o that was the reason I can speak so accurately minutes.

MENT.

f, in calling notice he had ded to enter , the results used measures ship then re-stions in re-Short Time spoke a few egulating the rvancy. He the Ministry mpotency on shop Burnett han a Minis-s address of

the Adminis-e charges of upon the pre-had been as osing. After and particu-f towns, his nts, and ad-and Catholic might be pro-ent weakness are.

the motion e House ad-

er Members, o which the

s.

ate on the Mr. HUME il the follow-

l RUSSELL, ok part, Mr. y of 63 to 18, e on the Bill. preamble fol-was adjd.

r proceedings ter, &c., Bill sued any in-round of em-he felt, after usillanimous as to display hich was im-an then made leniber of the g Lord Mor-the Attorney-ly.

report of the had only just uld show that ops Bill" the

ressure of the

he entire his-gland, which 430, and from d by request-go into Com-scussion, was m withdrawn,

had time to , moved the establishing a vision ensued, ndment, 14; were ordered

ent, the effect cate the true

on upon that omission; for Mr. Aglionby, Wortley, Mr. vho, however, l to leave out ld consent to n which, how) hearty laugh, dministration

The image of George and James Bradley on trial for the murder of John Riley (*Sheffield & Rotherham Independent*, 24 July 1847)

serving half his sentence and be returned to this country on good behaviour. The ticket of leave system was not a popular one as it meant having criminals free in the community, but others felt it was a more humane way of treating prisoners. J.P. Bean tells us that the system of transportation fell out of use for a while, but this is something that Mr Wilson Overend, who had examined both brothers, was very much against and he believed that transportation should be re-introduced and it should be for life. This case indicates the way that tradesmen of the city were in danger from highway robbers and thieves. The late opening hours would have been a godsend to people prepared to lie in wait for their prey. But more insidious were the domestic murders in one's own home.

Chapter Five

⟫·◈·⟪

Inflicted after Death

The citizens of Sheffield in May 1851 were intrigued by the opening of the Great
Exhibition at the Crystal Palace in London. Descriptions of the opening itself and the
layout of the exhibits were in the local newspapers of the time. The Great Exhibition
was an unparalleled statement of the Victorian attitude that Britain was a nation that
excelled in leading the world in industrial and cultural expansion. Some of the leading
manufacturers of Sheffield were included in the exhibition in a section known as the
Sheffield Court. Queen Victoria and Prince Albert let it be known that they would be
inspecting the court with the Prince and Princess of Prussia on 17 May 1851. Models
of some of the steelworks were on show and they visited the model of Messrs Naylor
Vickers & Company to see the steel production with specimens of steel in its various
stages. It seems that Queen Victoria was:

> Most gracious and calculated to remove entirely the embarrassment which persons
> unaccustomed to appear before Royalty might naturally feel in her presence. Prince Albert
> showed a degree of acquaintance with the art and manufacture of the Country, which was
> most gratifying.
>
> (*Sheffield & Rotherham Independent*, 17 May 1851)

Even the ten-year-old Edward, Prince of Wales attended a few days later with his tutor,
Mr Birch, where he spent a considerable time among the models of the machinery
and showed 'much liveliness and intelligence'.

The readers of the Sheffield newspapers would have read copiously the details of the
visit of the Queen to the Great Exhibition and it must have given the citizens great pride
to know of Her Majesty's interest in the products of the city of Sheffield. Prince Albert had
been as instrumental in the building of the Crystal Palace as he was in the modernization
of Buckingham Palace. It is probable that very few homes in Sheffield, however, were
able to be modernized and include inside toilet facilities. Many houses were built around
yards and courtyards with communal toilets known as privies. Individual toilets were

The crowded courts at the rear of Duke Street. (Sheffield Local Studies Library)

often shared by as many as twenty people. It was inside one of these privies where Mrs Eliza Wilkinson said that she had hidden in the early hours of Sunday 4 May 1851.

At 2 a.m. on Sunday morning Mr and Mrs Lund of Wilson's Yard off Duke Street Sheffield Park heard someone throwing pebbles up to the window. These courtyards were so numerous they were often just given numbers, as the map of 1890 will illustrate. Mrs Lund went to the window to discover her neighbour, Mrs Wilkinson, aged twenty-five, standing barefoot in the yard. Her neighbour asked her if she could come in as she had quarrelled with her husband, John, and he had threatened to slit her throat. As a consequence of this she had jumped out of the bedroom window to escape him. Mrs Lund opened the front door and Wilkinson came in. She was shivering. Mrs Lund offered to light a candle, but she told her that she would be alright; she was just cold as she had spent the last two hours in the privy hiding from her husband. Mrs Lund left her by the hearth and went upstairs to bed. The following morning when Mrs Lund awoke she found that Wilkinson had let herself out and had gone across the yard to a neighbour, Mrs Johnson, as soon as she saw that she was moving about downstairs. When Mrs Johnson opened the door, Wilkinson started to cry as she repeated the story of the row the previous night. When Mrs Johnson asked her why she hadn't called her she said that she had thrown pebbles at her window about midnight but she could not make her and her husband hear her. Mrs Johnson said that was strange as her and her husband had both been in and out of the yard about 12 a.m. but had heard or seen nothing out of the ordinary.

Wilkinson then stated that she wished that she had her boots, which were in the house, and asked Mrs Johnson to get them for her. Mrs Johnson tried the door but it appeared to be locked. In actual fact it was 'snecked' in such a way that it could only be opened from the inside. Mr Wilkinson was in the habit of snecking the door on his way out to work in a morning whilst the rest of the family were still in bed. She said that her husband was due to go to work early as he was a carter and had to attend to his employer, Mr Quible's, horses. Mrs Johnson returned to her neighbour's door and shouted to Wilkinson's daughter, Ann, to open the front door and let herself and her mother into the house. The child came down from the garret where she slept and opened the door. Wilkinson pushed her way into the house where she went straight through the kitchen into the middle room. Entering the room she turned and called Mrs Johnson to 'come and see'. Mrs Johnson entered and saw the body of John Wilkinson, aged thirty-four, lying face down on the floor, covered with blood that was coming from a wound in his neck.

'Oh he has murdered himself!' Wilkinson cried.

The police were sent for and Wilkinson went to Mrs Johnson, who tried her best to comfort the poor girl. She sent Ann to fetch an aunt named Zell to the house, telling her that 'John had murdered himself by cutting his throat'. A constable named James Rogers was dispatched to the house. The Victorian police were ignorant of the need to protect a crime scene, as was evident when he moved the body away from the pool of blood and tried to loosen the man's neckerchief in order to examine the neck wound. He then proceeded to wash the face and hands of the deceased. In the house were a next-door neighbour, Thomas Johnson, and the landlord of the property, Mr Wilson.

PC Rogers said that the wounds had been inflicted with a knife, and a white-handled knife was found by Mr Wilson and handed to him. Without washing his own hands, which were now covered in blood, he grasped the knife, contaminating the evidence. He asked Mr Johnson and Mr Wilson to leave and ensuring that the rest of the house was empty, he locked the door and went to report to his superiors. He reported that it was a case of suicide when he got back to the Town Hall. Superintendent Raynor quickly sent two more experienced officers to the house to investigate further.

Inspectors Astwood and Linley immediately noted that this was not a suicide but a scene of foul play. They turned the body over and examined the wound in the neck, which had been caused after death to make it look like suicide. Clumps of hair had been torn out of the victim's head and the back of his head was crushed by severe blows. A knife was found under a stool with the name 'J. Fieldsend' on it, which was later identified by the lodger, William Battersby, a cousin to Mrs Wilkinson, as belonging to him. The knife was described as being so old and fragile that the wound could not have been inflicted on a man who was struggling for his life. They examined the kitchen and parlour and found blood splattered all over the walls and the ceiling of the two rooms. A curious poker was found in the fireplace among the ashes, the end of which had been flattened and turned up about $1 - 1 \frac{1}{2}$ inches in order to make a fire rake. Remains of the supper were on the table, consisting of a piece of beef, a pound of butter and some milk. All had splashes of blood on them. In the flue over the fire was found a man's worsted stocking with blood on the soles of the feet and under the oven was the other stocking of the pair, also with blood on it. This stocking had been partially burnt. Going upstairs they noted that the bedroom window which Wilkinson had claimed to have jumped out of was closed and fastened. On the windowsill was a small piece of lead and some house plants neatly arranged. There was no sign of any disturbance, which there should have been had someone jumped the 12ft into the yard. In the attic bedroom, which was shared by Battersby and Ann, the daughter, they found a man's shirt and trousers. When Mrs Lund told Wilkinson that the police had taken some clothing belonging to Battersby, she asked if there had been any blood found on the clothing as he had cut his finger on the Thursday night. The two inspectors sent for Wilkinson, who was still at the neighbour's house, and they questioned her.

She told them that the previous night she had met her husband in town at eleven o'clock and they had walked home. As Wilkinson went to her house, her husband had gone into the nearby grocer's shop which was still open and whilst there, his daughter appeared and they walked home together. All four ate some supper and then Ann went to bed. She later told the court that when she went upstairs she left her parents downstairs and Battersby was washing himself at the kitchen sink. Wilkinson told the inspectors that Battersby had left at 11.30 p.m. to go to Belph, near Whitwell, as his sister had called during the day asking him to call at his parents' house. She described the row she had with her husband when he told her that he wanted to buy a new coat and she asked him not to buy one just yet, to make do with the old one for a while, and he started to quarrel with her saying that he would 'do her in'. She became frightened when he grabbed hold of a razor and threatened her with it and so she ran up to the bedroom and jumped out of the bedroom window. After failing to arouse Mrs Johnson, she had crept into the toilet where she stayed for two hours. Only when she could stand the cold no longer and she was sure that Wilkinson had gone to sleep did she wake Mr and Mrs Lund.

The two inspectors then spoke to the neighbours. The next-door neighbour, Mr Thomas Johnson, told them that he had been disturbed the previous night about five minutes past midnight when he heard noises from next door which he described as a rumbling of furniture, like someone moving tables and chairs. He opened the window but saw nothing. After a few moments the noises stopped and he went back to bed. Another neighbour on the other side, Mary Sarah Pearson, who lived with her parents and slept in the attic of the house, said she too had been disturbed by the noise of furniture being moved. She also heard the sound of a heavy object falling downstairs and then someone running down the stairs. She also heard someone run into the yard and the footsteps sounded like someone with boots or shoes on by the clatter that they made on the cobbles. The Lunds described the previous night's events to the two inspectors and told them that they had never known John Wilkinson to be 'in a passion' but that the description would more easily suit the temperament of his wife. On the contrary, they saw him as a quiet and good-tempered man.

Elizabeth Johnson, the wife of Samuel Johnson, who lived opposite, had known the deceased man for about nine months. She also described the events, stating that Wilkinson had come to her house at 7.15 a.m. that morning. She told the two inspectors how the body was found, almost as if Wilkinson was expecting it to be there. When they asked her about the condition of Wilkinson upon finding the body of her husband, she told them that she appeared to be 'fretting' and had said to several persons that she 'wished that she had stayed in the house and he had killed her too'. Then Mrs Johnson dropped a bombshell. She told the police that she had heard the Wilkinsons rowing and the reason had been that John thought that his wife was becoming too friendly with Battersby. At this point it was agreed that Wilkinson's story was very suspicious and she was taken to the Town Hall to report to Superintendent Raynor. He quickly dispatched Inspector Linley to Belph, estimated to be approximately fourteen miles from Sheffield, to arrest Battersby. He went there and met Battersby's father in the lane leading to the house and asked him if he had seen his son. Both parents denied seeing him for the past few weeks, although they had been expecting him to arrive on Sunday when he wasn't working. Linley searched the parents' house but no one else was there. Speaking to neighbours he found that although Battersby had not been to visit his parents, he had been seen twice in the neighbourhood at 9 a.m. and 11 a.m. Although the inspector returned back to Sheffield empty handed Battersby, when he heard the police were looking for him, also arrived back in Sheffield and was found in the house of a neighbour, where he was arrested and taken to the Town Hall.

The inquest on the body of John Wilkinson was held on Tuesday 6 May 1851 at the Town Hall in front of the coroner. It was noted that crowds of people thronged the streets around Wilson's Yard, such was the curiosity and notoriety which had been aroused by the case. Before the enquiry started, the jury went to the house of the deceased to view the body. The first witness was the daughter of the murdered man,

Ann Wilkinson, who was described by the reporter as being a 'very intelligent child'. The coroner examined her carefully about the meaning of the oath and after being reassured that she understood the need to tell the truth, she gave evidence. She said that her parents had sometimes quarrelled and that there had been a row about a coat which her father wanted to buy. She was asked if they had ever argued about anything else and she said that on one occasion her mother wanted to go into town with Battersby but her father wouldn't allow it. He had told her that she was 'too friendly with Battersby'. She described the last time they had all eaten together ,when her mother and father had returned back to the house, and they had shared supper. The coroner asked her if she thought her parents had been drinking, but she said no, that they were both sober. She was asked if she heard Battersby go to bed, but she said that she had fallen asleep and did not know if he had come upstairs. She then described being awoken the next morning by Mrs Johnson's calls up to the attic window.

The post-mortem had been undertaken by Mr J. Farewell Wright, who told the jury that he had undertaken it on the orders of the coroner on the previous evening in the company of other surgeons. He had found that across the throat there was a cut of 2in in length which had severed the windpipe. The wounds to the throat were not the cause of death, and had been inflicted afterwards. Several extensive wounds were found on the back of the head, of which two or three were of an irregular form from 1 – 3in long. As a result of this attack the skull was extensively fractured. The stomach was healthy and had contained undigested food; the bladder, kidneys, intestines and liver were all perfectly healthy. When asked by the coroner if any of the injuries could have been self-inflicted, Mr Wright stated that they couldn't. The wounds in the head had been caused by repeated blows from a heavy instrument. Another surgeon,

Howard Street as it looks today. (Chris Drinkall)

Mr Carr of Howard Street, concurred with the results of the post-mortem and suggested that the injuries to the deceased were consistent with being attacked by the strange poker which had been found in the house. At this point, the coroner requested that as it was too late to hear any more depositions that the inquest be adjourned until the following Thursday afternoon.

Inspector Linley was the first person to give evidence at the resumed inquest on 8 May. He spoke of the search he had made of the property and particularly the window from where Wilkinson alleged that she had jumped. He had found that not only was the window closed but a blind was pulled down and the plants undisturbed. He felt that the piece of lead he found on the windowsill would have stuck to the skirt of anyone jumping out of the window and therefore he felt that Wilkinson was not telling the truth about her exit from the house. In the statement that she made at the Town Hall, Wilkinson said that her husband had been out of humour all week and when she objected to him buying the coat he had flown into a passion, saying to her that 'he will be the death of her before morning'. She told Linley that he had previously tried to commit suicide by throwing himself into the river at Tinsley. William Battersby had said that the couple were quarrelling when he left the house to go to his parents. When asked which was the route he took, he said that he went up the park through Mosbrough, leaving Eckington to the right-hand side and thence to Barlborough and through Whitwell to Belph. He had seen no one on the journey apart from a man called Joseph Hall, who he had seen at a distance. He stated that he had cut his knuckles on the previous Saturday and that had caused the blood to be found on his trousers. Also, as part of his job as a porter on the railway, he had to transport barrels of blood and therefore they could be the reason why blood had been found on his clothes. Inspector Linley had asked Joseph Hall if he had seen Battersby and he said that he had seen a man about 5 a.m. on the morning of Sunday 4 May, but did not know the name of the man. Battersby had told Linley that he had slept in a hayloft of a beerhouse on the Sunday night at Barlborough. When he finally went to see his parents at Belph he had been told that the police were looking for him and he came back to Sheffield to give himself up.

After all the evidence had been heard and the statements recorded, it was usual for the prisoners to attend the inquest and give their version of events, but Superintendent Raynor stated that he had orders from the Chairman of the West Riding Quarter Sessions, Mr Wilson Overend, that the prisoners were not allowed to be present at the inquest. He pointed out that it was the jury's duty to give the verdict on the cause of death, not the fate of the prisoners. This was not the first time the Mr Overend had taken these actions. In the inquest on the body of Caleb Barker of Swinton in January 1847, he had forbidden the attendance of the suspect, Garland. The coroner was so incensed that he wrote to the Home Secretary. The Home Secretary, however, stated that he had no authority for denying the prisoners to be brought before the jury. The coroner at the Wilkinson inquest resented the inference, stating that:

> in his opinion the rights of justice are frustrated by the collisions between the magistrate and the coroner. It had been his practice to hold these courts in the presence of the accused.

He had been a coroner for 21 years and had considerable experience in these matters. For the sake of the prisoners he did not want the jury asking questions which may lead to an admission which might incriminate themselves.

A discussion followed where it was suggested that the jury form a deputation to attend Mr Overend and ask him why he had not permitted the two people to attend the inquest, but the jury soon abandoned this idea. The room was cleared and after a consultation of one and a half hours, the jury brought in a verdict of guilty against William Battersby as the principle and Eliza Wilkinson as the accessory for aiding and assisting to murder John Wilkinson. Still complaining about his treatment by Mr Overend, the coroner wrote out the warrant for committal to York Castle, to which the prisoners were dispatched the following day. The trial took place on 23 July 1851 under Mr Justice Williams. The excitement of the case ensured that the court was full and throughout the day the side galleries were crowded.

The judge, aware of the difficulties for a child giving evidence against her parent, requested that she sit at the side of him to give her statement, which she did, adding only that all the adults in the house had taken their boots off before supper which was in itself most irregular. The clerk read out the charges, to which the pair replied 'not guilty'. But the pair were doomed from the start; the amount of evidence against them was overwhelming. In his summing up, the judge noted the curious time that Battersby had decided to go to see his parents in the middle of the night. He pointed out that as an employee of the railway he could have quite easily made his way to the station, approximately four miles from Belph, at a much more suitable hour. He estimated that it would have taken him four or five hours to have sufficient time to walk the distance. Wilkinson had said that Battersby had left the house at 11 p.m. but the shopkeeper had noted the time that John Wilkinson and his daughter were still in the shop at that time and it was 11.20 p.m. before they went out and the four people still had to have supper together. The judge pointed out to the jury that in this case there was a lack of motive for the crime and that both suspects had an appearance of innocence up to the point of the death. There might have been some provocation and if there was any doubt in any of the jury's minds they would have to acquit them of the lesser verdict. The jury now retired at 7.10 p.m. The trial had been going on since 9 a.m. and perhaps this was the reason they only took half an hour to return. There was absolute silence as the verict of manslaughter was given. The judge stated that:

This crime approaches so nearly to the crime of murder that I should be deserting my duty if I did not subject you to the punishment next in the degree of severity to that which would have been your fate if you had been found guilty of willful murder.

He then sentenced them both to transportation for life. Neither prisoner had displayed any emotion during the trial, but Wilkinson swooned on hearing the sentence and was carried from the dock. This harsh sentence reflected the severity of the crime which appalled most of the crowd. Indeed, when the prisoners went out of the courtroom and into the yard around York Castle there was a crowd of people, no doubt many from Sheffield, assembled in the grounds. When the male prisoner was placed in a cab people hooted and shouted, indicating the strong feelings of disgust and horror against the couple. When it was realized that the female prisoner had yet to come out of the building, the crowd swarmed back into the yard and met her coming out with two prison officers and they booed her until she was safely locked in the prison. The young ages of the prisoners meant not only that their sentence would be a long one, but also it would ensure that they would never see their home town, indeed England, ever again. The sentence of transportation was becoming more popular and J.P. Bean tells us that between 1788 and 1868, 162,000 men, women and children, some as young as seven years of age, were transported to Australia and Tasmania for crimes ranging from murder, burglary and pick-pocketing.

But that was not the end of the story. A later joint confession was printed in the local newspaper during the week of 2 August 1847 when the *Sheffield & Rotherham Independent* stated that when the child, Ann, had gone to bed, John Wilkinson had gone out into the yard for a few minutes. On his return he found Battersby's arm around his wife. He tried to suggest to Wilkinson that he was just fooling around and trying to take her handkerchief off her, but it was too much for Wilkinson. He threatened, 'I'll have no more of it. We've had too much of it already'. Turning to his wife he threatened 'I'll kill thee' and raised a knife. Battersby tried to take the knife but did not succeed and in an attempt to protect the woman, he hit John Wilkinson on the head with a poker. Mrs Wilkinson picked up another poker and hit him on the arm until he dropped the knife. He fell to the floor and they both beat him till he was dead. She then alleged that she jumped out of the window and Battersby, no doubt advised by Wilkinson, cut the throat of the deceased man in an attempt to make it look like suicide. No doubt this story was an approximation of the truth in the hope that it would lead to a lesser sentence, but the truthfulness of the couple has to be doubted due to their constant lying in the story they had told so far.

Crimes of passion were not scarce in a city like Sheffield, nor were drunken brawls which led to death. The next two cases took place in the barracks at Sheffield and involved soldiers who lied in order to save their skins.

Chapter Six

⟾◈⟽

The Barracks Murders

The life of a soldier can be very dangerous and, as a result, many form deep bonds with members of their regiment when on the battlefield. Many brave actions have saved the lives of others and, as a consequence, ranks tend to close together when threatened by outsiders or civilians. The barracks at Sheffield was home to the 40th Regiment of Foot, but in October 1847 they also had another regiment stationed with them, the 4th Dragoons. Both these battalions had been involved in the American War of Independence from 1777-1782 and had fought bravely in the many battles between Britain and the different states of America, formerly seen as a British colony, the different states uniting to become United States of America. The uniforms of the foot regiments were grey coats and hats, but the horse regiment of the 4th Dragoons were better known for their red cloaks and caps. The following case is one which is probably not listed in the annals of the regiments, as it is full of lies and discrepancies and it doesn't help that most of the parties were drunk. However, the twist in the tale is worthy of Agatha Christie.

On the evening of Saturday 11 November a group of people were having a night out in the Army Hotel near Walkley. At some time between 12 a.m. and 1 a.m. it was decided that they would make their way home to Infirmary Lane where the party would continue. The group consisted of John Morton, George and Maria Roberts, Aaron Dickinson and Thomas Simmonite. John's brother, Thomas, got up to go with them as they were leaving, but, being rather inebriated, fell behind the rest of the group. As they approached Barrack Lane they heard some men singing and were confronted by two soldiers, described as foot soldiers. The men were drunk and celebrating the fact that they had both been given a night off. They had been drinking and had gone to the Barrack Hotel, but finding it closed had proceeded to have the outdoor concert. The group passed and they heard Thomas Morton urge the two soldiers to be quiet as it was late at night and when Mrs Roberts turned round, she saw that a scuffle had broke out between Thomas and the two men. She noted that a man fell to the ground and she shouted for the nightwatchman. Suddenly two guards came out of the nearby

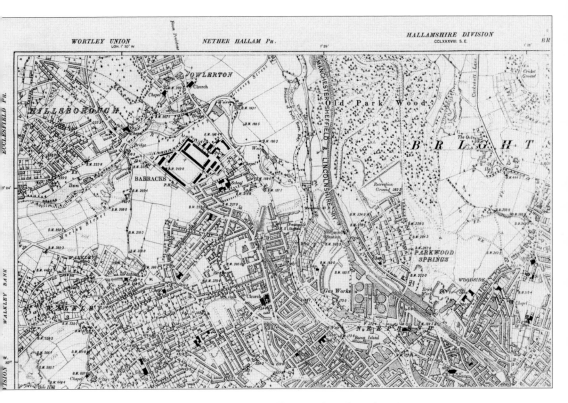

A map showing the Sheffield Barracks in 1924. (Sheffield Local Studies Library)

barracks and rushed over to the scene. She told the inquest that the two men were wearing grey overcoats and hats. Two more soldiers followed who were wearing the red cloaks. The foot soldiers had rifles and bayonets at the end. Mrs Roberts saw one of the soldiers knock Morton down, but she could not be sure which soldier it was as the four others were now gathered around the body and several were kicking him. Mr Roberts stated that he had been drinking all day and admitted that he was somewhat fresh when he gave his account of what had happened that night. One of the soldiers had threatened to run him through until another soldier shouted that 'he was not the one they were after'. John Morton was carrying some ale in a jug for the following party and as he bent down to put the jug on the floor, one of the soldiers grabbed him by the hair and held him down. He managed to get away and went a short distance where he could still see the affray. Mrs Roberts continued to shout for the watch. Only when the nightwatchman appeared did John Morton go back to the group to find it was his own brother that was on the floor and he was bleeding profusely. They managed to carry the badly wounded man back to the Army Hotel, where he was obviously in a very bad state. Thomas Morton was moved to the hospital where he was attended by doctors until the early hours of Sunday 25 September without regaining consciousness.

The nightwatchman, William Thorpe, told the inquest that he had pulled one of the soldiers off the body of the man, asking the soldier if he intended to murder him.

The soldier replied that he had been insulted. His belt had been left on the floor and, without a word, his comrade picked it up and they began walking back to the barracks. The first man was a sergeant and he insisted that Thorpe give the man up to him as this was a military matter and would be dealt with by the proper authorities. Thorpe asked for his name and he gave it as Sergeant Thompson and Thorpe gave the man up into his custody.

Charles Johnson, a corporal in the 40th Foot Regiment, was on duty that night. He knew that two men, Dominic Mulrannon and Joseph Rennison, had been given the night off and were celebrating their freedom. At 1.20 a.m. he heard Private Patrick Flannery call to him that there was a disturbance outside the barracks. Dominic Mulrannon had rushed into the barracks shouting that some civilians were murdering Rennison. Johnson called out to two privates, John Johnson and John Green, and ordered them to take off their bayonets. When they returned he ordered them to take Rennison to the guard room and to keep him there. When he asked Rennison what happened, he told him that they had been attacked by a group of civilians and knocked down. He had fought as best as he could but was taken by the watch.

An inquest was held on the body of Thomas Morton on Friday 1 October 1847. At this point, two or three soldiers were in custody and, at the orders of Mr Overend, were not allowed to attend the inquest. This placed the coroner in a dilemma. As we have seen, this was not usual practice. He felt it not right or just that evidence should be given in the absence of the accused parties. At the inquest, the evidence of Private Patrick Flannery was heard. He described hearing the disturbance and upon reaching the group heard one of the civilians call out to another to 'strike him for a bloody squaddie'. Mulrannon shouted that Rennison was being attacked. After the affray was over, Rennison picked up the belt and threw it down in the guard room and went to his own room. Flannery was asked by the coroner if any of the horse soldiers in their red cloaks had been involved in the fighting and he told him no, that 'no horse guards had gone out whilst I was there'.

Dr Hugh Mellor, surgeon of Owlerton, was called at 2 a.m. on Sunday 12 September, but he was ill and so his brother went in his absence. He found the deceased insensible. He had a compound fracture on the posterior part of the skull, two fractured ribs, contusions on both arms and a split lip. Further contusions were noted on the right side of his head. He attended Morton from Sunday to Friday 24 September. He told the jury that he knew that it was doubtful that the deceased would recover as the man was not in sound health and his lungs were diseased. He gave the opinion that the cause of death was a fractured skull caused by the stock of a gun and, in his opinion, it would require a heavy blow to achieve such a wound.

Dr Samuel Gregory, surgeon, called to see the deceased on the previous Saturday to attend to him. He said that, 'I found him very ill and beginning to sink. I attended him all the night before his death'. On Monday the 13th he, with Dr Hugh and Dr Charles Mellor and Mr Gledhill held a post-mortem on the body of Thomas Morton. They found that his lungs were affected by grinder's disease (a term which we now call silicosis). The left kidney contained a lot of pus. They attributed his death to 'the injuries received on the head and body to which his constitution sank under the

now. Exchequer-bills are pat to 3s. premium. Bank Stock for Account is 196. No one seems inclined to do business.
Spanish Three per Cents. are 28, and Portuguese Four per Cents., 23; Brazil Stock, ex. dividend, is 78; Dutch Two-and-a-Half per Cents. are 54 to 55.
Railway Shares have been lower, as a matter of course, and it is, perhaps, a consolation that they can be sold at all just now.

MAN KILLED IN AN AFFRAY WITH SOLDIERS.

Yesterday afternoon, an inquest was held at the Army Hotel, Hill foot, on view of the body of Thomas Morton, whose death was occasioned by injuries received in an affray with two soldiers of the 40th Regiment of Foot. The evidence given before the Jury was of the most conflicting character, and is detailed at length below.

The Coroner said, they were summoned to enquire how and in what manner Thomas Morton, the deceased, came to his death. He understood that he had died from some injuries received upon the head late on the night of Saturday, the 11th inst, or early on Sunday morning. They would have to enquire under what circumstances, and by whose hands the injuries were inflicted. In the course of the examination, it might be necessary to draw their attention more particularly to the evidence, but their first duty was to view the body. He believed that two or three soldiers, suspected of having committed the violence, were in custody at the Town-Hall; but he was afraid they would not be able to have these parties before them, or to close the enquiry that day.

Mr. T. W. Rodgers, solicitor, begged, at the request of the officers stationed at the Barracks, to be allowed to watch the proceedings, as he understood that some men belonging to their regiment were to be implicated in the enquiry. He could only say that it was the wish of the officers that the most strict investigation should be made into the matter, and they should feel it their duty to afford all the assistance they could. The matter was one affecting the soldiers, who had a right to look in some degree to their officers for protection if deserving it, and if they were not deserving of that protection, they felt that it was their duty, as public officers of the land, that the Jury should have every information which could be afforded.

Mr. A. C. Branson claimed the privilege, on behalf the friends of the deceased, to watch the proceedings.

The Coroner said, he should, in this instance, adopt his usual course of conducting the enquiry openly and publicly.

The following witnesses were then examined :—

Maria, wife of George Roberts, of Infirmary lane, edge-tool grinder, deposed : I knew Thomas Morton, the deceased. On Saturday night, the 11th, I went to the Army Hotel to my husband, who was there. I sat in the bar till my husband was ready to go home. Thomas Morton was in the bar. I and my husband left there between twelve and one o'clock, accompanied by John Morton, Aaron Dickinson, and another man, whose name I do not know. We left Thomas Morton in the house, but he followed us out immediately, and walked about ten yards behind us. When we were just turning the corner of the Barrack lane, we heard some one singing. When we got up to them, and just at the corner, we saw they were two foot soldiers. John Morton asked them what they were singing songs for on Sunday morning. More words passed between them, which I did not hear. The two soldiers and John Morton began scuffling

A report on the inquest of Thomas Morton. (*Sheffield & Rotherham Independent*, 2 October 1847)

injuries'. The coroner asked him if, in his opinion, the man would have survived his injuries if he had been in a better state of health, but he said that he would not, 'His injuries to his head had caused his death'.

At this point the coroner agreed that no more evidence would be heard from other men at the barracks as they agreed in principle that no arms had been evident on that evening. The inquest was adjourned for an hour in order for the jury to have some refreshments. When the inquest started once more, the coroner was still upset at what he saw as the interference of Mr Overend. He told the jury that witnesses were at that very moment being examined by Mr Overend and that:

> The problems that this caused to the present inquest can not be described sufficiently. To have two courts sitting at the same time was a slight to his experienced and professional way of operating. It is not right that new magistrates finding a new law which magistrates who have been on the bench for many years have been unable to find out and which caused such chaos with the processes of the law.

The foreman of the jury stood up and pointed out that there had been many discrepancies between the evidence presented and asked that Aaron Dickenson be sent for to clarify matters, as he was the one who was most sober of the group and who had given the clearest evidence so far. The request was complied with and Dickenson of Broad Street once again went through his evidence. He stated that it was Thomas Morton who had attacked one of the soldiers about the singing and in the scuffle

Broad Street as it looks today. (Chris Drinkall)

had fallen onto the floor. Of the four soldiers, he noted three soldiers in grey and one in the red cap and cloak of the horse soldiers and that two of them had guns and 'something glittering on the end' but he could not say what they were. He witnessed two of them strike Morton with their guns. He told the coroner that at this point he spoke to Simmonite and they both agreed to have nothing more to do with the affray and they both went home.

Mr Rogers, who was a solicitor acting on behalf of the soldiers in the barracks, asked the coroner if he could address the jury. He told them that:

> Witnesses for the prosecution have entirely exculpated the soldiers who had been kept in custody for having inflicted any injuries which caused the deceased's death. There was nothing more than a scuffle between Rennison and Mulrannon until the guards stated to have arms with them came out of the barracks. It had been proven that the prisoners did not have any arms with them which could have been inflicted on the deceased with the barrel of a gun. It is therefore considered that the prisoners could have nothing to do with injuries which caused the death, but rather it was caused by the guards.

He added that there was a great mystery over this case, but his clients could not help the jury with it. The coroner summed up the evidence that the deceased had come to his death by violence inflicted on him by someone under circumstances of manslaughter. It was for the jury to decide who did it. If Mulrannon or Rennison did not themselves inflict the wounds, then the wounds were inflicted by other people who did nothing to stop the attack. Therefore, all the parties involved were guilty of manslaughter. The jury returned a verdict of manslaughter on Dominic Mulrannon, Joseph Rennison, John Johnson and Joseph Green and all four were to be committed to York.

The Winter Assizes were held on 18 December 1847 and instead of the four men that had been charged with manslaughter, two different men were now in the dock. It seems that after being committed to the Assizes, Dominic Mulrannon confessed that in actual fact he had witnessed the two men, Flannery and Dalton, coming out of the barracks with muskets and saw them kill Thomas Morton. He spoke out when the verdict of manslaughter had been given to himself and three other innocent men who had nothing to do with the crime. The following week the trial started and Patrick Flannery, aged twenty-one, and John Dalton, aged twenty-two, were charged with the manslaughter of Thomas Morton.

The prisoners, surprisingly, were undefended. When asked how they pleaded, Dalton replied that he was not guilty and Flannery made a long rambling statement about being on guard at the time of the attack. Mr Overend, appearing for the prosecution, said that the enquiries had resulted in proceedings against these two men and the four others were to be dismissed. The judge requested that the four men be formally discharged in order that they may be allowed to give evidence at the trial, which was done. Mrs Rogers was called and it seems that her memory had been clearer during the interim as she now spoke of one of the guards lifting his rifle to strike Morton. She stated that, 'I saw him strike Morton more than once'. She did not see anyone else strike him, although admitted that she could not identify the man who had inflicted the injuries.

Dominic Mulrannon was next to give evidence. He said that he was a private in the 40th Regiment of Foot stationed in Sheffield and that Flannery was a fellow member of his regiment, whilst Dalton was with the horse regiment of Dragoons. He said that on the night he had been singing, Morton was attacked by Rennison and he fell. When Mulrannon went to lift Morton up, he struck Mulrannon. He witnessed Dalton strike him with his gun and then he saw Flannery strike him over the ribs or thighs. Mulrannon asked him to stop before he killed the man and told him that the watch was on it's way and he had better go. Flannery begged him 'for Gods sake don't tell them I was there or I will get twelve months'. Rennison next appeared in the dock and corroborated Mulrannon's account.

The jury retired to bring a verdict in this most difficult of cases. Lies and deceit had been part of the trial and it was hard to know who the guilty parties really were. After three hours, the jury came back into court and the foreman gave the verdict that it had been impossible to decide and, as a consequence, they had to release both men as being not guilty. The under-gaoler at the castle in York reported that Dalton was in a very bad state of health and could not be discharged without a medical certificate. It also appeared that neither man had any money and therefore it was agreed that the men would be discharged on Monday when arrangements could be made for Dalton to be examined by the surgeon and the military authorities would make arrangements for the men to be returned to the barracks in Sheffield.

The Sheffield Barracks hit the headlines once again in March 1861 when an attack by a soldier towards his commanding officer surprised most of the inhabitants of the barracks.

Private George Smith was known to be a moody and violent man who often used to abuse his wife. Nowadays the Army takes a strong stance on such behaviour but in the Victorian era wife abuse was something which had to be dealt with by the husband. Religious belief of the period held the view that it was necessary for a wife to be subjugated to her husband and that he was responsible for chastising her, no doubt encouraging such behaviour. Sergeant William Austin was a man ahead of his time and when he heard evidence that Smith had ill-used his wife, he brought it to the attention of the military authorities. As a result of this, Smith was sentenced to be confined to barracks for a few days. Smith festered on his revenge, uttering threats regarding taking the life of either Austin or his wife. On Tuesday 5 March 1861, Smith met Sergeant Austin about 5.30 p.m. as Austin was heading home to take tea with his wife in the married quarters of the barracks. Smith asked him a trivial question regarding his duty and then went to his own quarters, where he took a rifle.

He proceeded to the quarters where the sergeant and his wife were having tea and burst into the room. He raised the rifle to his shoulder and aimed directly at Austin's chest. Guessing his intention, his wife tried to put herself in between Smith and Austin and at the same time Austin turned sideways out of the chair. Smith fired once. The sound was so loud that another soldier, Private George Goodland, ran into the room and tried to overpower Smith, who was desperately trying to reload the rifle for another shot at his victim. Thankfully he was overpowered and taken to the guardroom. On the way he asked the sergeant escorting him, 'Is Austin dead?' and he expressed some remorse that he had not done a better job of finishing the man off. Austin was taken to the infirmary where he was examined by the barracks' surgeon. He was found to have a superficial wound in his neck, the ball of the rifle having grazed his neck and carried away skin and part of the muscle underneath. The barracks surgeon said that Austin should have recovered sufficiently to be able to testify at the court in two weeks time. The military authorities would have preferred to have kept the matter within the military arena, but they were unable to as it was now a civil matter and handed Smith over to the police force on 10 March.

A trial was held at the Police Courts of the Town Hall on 13 March. George Smith was charged with shooting with attempt to murder William Austin. The evidence of the witnesses were heard and it was noted that George Smith showed no remorse and claimed that he had been drunk and had no recollection of what happened. The jury took no time at all to send him for trial at the next Assizes. George Smith received the death sentence for the cruel and calculated way he had tried to take not only a man's life, but a fellow soldier to boot.

Chapter Seven

━━━◆◈◆━━━

The Cruel Husband

It has to be said that many working class women living in the towns and cities of Britain were the subject of domestic violence. As we have seen, in Victorian society, women were seen as the man's property and any income she received would have to be handed over to him. She had no right over him, or any children she gave birth to. It was a hard time for women and they had very little recourse to help in a patriarchal society, despite the fact that there was a woman on the throne. J.P. Bean tells us that in the Victorian period women were systematically mistreated. In 1862 in Sheffield alone there were 240 summonses for assault on women and children. Ten years later there were 396. The problem was so dire that in a Town Council meeting in 1874 they demanded that the magistrates order flogging for such crimes. Such cases were reported in the local newspaper, as slowly changes were made and I would like to think that these cases were the bedrock for the rise of feminism. However, for the women in Sheffield in the Victorian era, help was generations away.

Cases of domestic violence were more prevalent in the working class areas of the town. Low class lodging houses and countless beerhouses were scattered throughout the town. These were places where poorer people congregated to live and to drink to escape the poverty and unsanitary conditions in which they were forced to exist. In many cases the male head of the lodging and beerhouses might have other employment and the day-to-day running of the establishment was the responsibility of his wife. The brutish lives which were led by the inmates of these places can only be imagined. Elizabeth Copestake was the wife of the master of such a house in Sims Court. Her husband, Thomas, aged forty-four, had been a police officer for the borough ten or eleven years previously but having left the police force three years before, he had opened up the lodging/beerhouse known to its users as the King William. It was described as being quite a large building, consisting of five bedrooms upstairs and four reception rooms downstairs. The front door was for the use of the customers and the back door for the family and lodgers' use.

A typical Sheffield brewery (Truswells) which supplied beer to the town. (Reproduced courtesy of Picture Sheffield)

Sims Court. Court No. 4, 1890. (Reproduced courtesy of Picture Sheffield)

A frequent victim of domestic violence, Elizabeth took refuge in alcohol and as a consequence of this she was carried to bed drunk at 7.30 p.m. on the night of Wednesday 9 August 1865 by two of the lodgers in the house. She had been supplied with gin against the specific wishes of her husband. Copestake had been out for most of the day and when he returned at about ten o clock in the evening, he was in a filthy temper. In the house was a little girl called Emily Rose, an orphan aged eleven who lived in the lodgings with her sister, Mrs Selina Kitson, and her husband. She gave Copestake the money she had collected from people who were buying beer and he took a candle and went upstairs to the bedroom where his wife was. About a quarter of an hour later he returned downstairs and asked Emily if she had heard a bump from the bedroom above. She told him that she had heard a small bump, but she wasn't sure what it was. Then, worrying about the whereabouts of her sister, Emily went out to look for her. Her sister, Selina Kitson, the wife of Charles Kitson, had lodged at the house for almost three weeks. She and another woman, Mrs Clara Hall, had first helped to get Elizabeth to bed and then both of them had gone out. When Copestake came back downstairs after seeing the condition in which his wife was in, he appeared to be quite agitated. Seeing Mr Charles Kitson in the bar of the house, he called to him and asked him to come and look at his wife. They both went upstairs and as Kitson entered the bedroom he saw the woman lying on the floor with so much blood on her face and around her mouth that he thought she had vomited the blood up. The left hand was under the body and the right hand was holding her hair. He thought that she had been punched and had said as much to Copestake, but he replied, 'It was not down to punching'. In his distracted state he wanted to fetch another neighbour, a woman named Mrs Ogley, and he asked Kitson to wait in the bedroom while he went to get her. Kitson, not wanting to remain in the room with the body of the woman, stood by the door, anxious to leave. Copestake then brought in Mrs Ann Ogley and showed her his wife's body that was still lying on the floor at the side of the bed. She was still alive and bleeding copiously from the head, he said to her, 'What do you think of this, Mrs Ogley?'

'It is a serious case; I wonder who's done it?' she replied.

He said, 'I don't know. I would give £5 to know who had done it'.

Ann Ogley bathed Mrs Copestake's head with water and put a cold cloth to the wound, but she did not respond and appeared insensible. Mrs Ogley thought that the wound had been inflicted some time before as the blood was matted in her hair. In her opinion it was not a fist that had made it, but that an instrument of some kind had been used. She was used to seeing bruises on the poor victim as the couple were often heard quarrelling.

Selina Kitson returned about 10.45 p.m. and found Copestake in the taproom. He told her that Elizabeth had been injured whilst falling out of bed. Mrs Kitson found this hard to believe as the bed was not that high and there was hardly any furniture to speak of in the room which could cause any injury. She wondered whether Elizabeth had fallen onto the chamber pot which was traditionally kept under the bed, but found this theory very hard to believe. She went up to see Elizabeth, but was unable to suggest what could have caused the injuries. At no time was a suggestion made that medical help be sought for the poor woman. The following day, Thursday 10 August, Copestake, suspecting that the Kitsons had given Elizabeth drugs, ordered all the family to get out of the house and never return. He told them 'that he had seen her drunk before but never so insensible that she can't get herself off the floor'. Later that day her brother, George West, visited the house at noon and asked Copestake, 'Is the missus in? Can I speak to her?' Copestake replied, 'Yes she is in and she is a bonny mess'.

West went upstairs and found his sister insensible. He felt that his sister was dying and he told Copestake that she was 'a murdered woman'. He asked him why he had not called the police or a doctor, reminding Copestake that he had been a policeman once and therefore he knew the procedure.

Copestake told him that he had been to fetch a doctor but he was out. West told him in no uncertain terms him to fetch another doctor as quickly as possible. Finally, at 1.40 p.m., Mr Edward M. Dibbs, a surgeon, arrived at the house and was taken to see the deceased. He had been led to believe that she had been drunk and had taken drugs. Therefore when he went to the house he fully expected to be investigating a case of poison and was astonished to find the woman showing signs of compression of the brain. She had a huge laceration on her head, which he told the court 'was 1 ½inches long and went right down to the bone'. By now the incident was being talked about in the town and Elizabeth's sister, Mrs Coward, arrived wanting to see her. She found Copestake in the kitchen and asked him what he had done this time.

'Nothing, she has been poisoned.' he replied.

'Who has poisoned her?' she asked.

He told her, 'I have some idea who has done it and would hunt the world through to find them out, for although I abused her I would not allow anyone else to do so'. Then he began to cry. Just then Mr Dibbs entered the kitchen and asked Copestake what had happened to Elizabeth. He told him that he had found her in that condition on the floor, halfway under the bed. Dibbs offered his opinion that she had been kicked. Copestake replied, 'A kick wouldn't do that'.

Mr Dibbs, lifting his feet up to indicate his own boots, said, 'These would not do that'. He told Copestake to lift up his own feet and, measuring his boots, stated, 'A boot like that would do it'.

On leaving the house, Mr Dibbs went to the Town Hall and spoke to the police constable on duty and expressed his grave concerns about the condition of the poor woman. Sergeant Bradbury found and arrested Copestake the same day, Thursday 10 August, at 7 p.m. at the bottom of King Street and he was charged with the assault of his wife. Mrs Coward stayed with her sister, who by now was having convulsions, but she never regained consciousness. The surgeon continued to visit the victim four times a day up to her death on Monday 14 at 12.40 p.m. No doubt Copestake was informed that upon her death the charge was no longer one of assault but now of a more serious charge.

An inquest was held on Tuesday 15 August at the Beehive Hotel, Glossop Road; before the coroner, Mr J. Webster Esq. The surgeon, Mr Dibbs, gave his evidence as to the state of the deceased woman. He described the bruising all around the wound on

The Beehive Hotel, Glossop Road. (Reproduced courtesy of Picture Sheffield)

her head, there was bruising on her left shoulder and on the lower part of her back and old bruises over other parts of her body. She had a bruise the size of the palm of his hand on her left hip and the finger of her right hand was slightly cut. He had completed the post-mortem that day and found that all her organs were healthy, there were no signs of poison in the stomach and the cause of death was the wound on her head. He gave his opinion that the bruise was caused by a blunt instrument. One of the jurors asked him if the wound could have been caused by the woman falling out of bed, but he stated that 'in his opinion that could not have been the cause of death because the bed was too low'. The same juror asked if a blunt instrument such as a boot could have caused the wound and Mr Dibbs gave his opinion that the wound resembled a kick from a boot.

The prisoner was called to give his statement, and he contradicted himself as to whether his wife was on the bed or not. He said that he returned home about ten o'clock and went upstairs, where he saw his wife on the bed. He turned her over to look in her pockets. The contents of the full day's takings of the beerhouse should have been in her pocket. He was in the habit of doing this since an incident four years previously, when she had once before been drugged and £4 had been taken out of her pocket. Another juror questioned whether someone intent on robbing her could have entered the front door of the lodging house and gone into the bedroom without being seen? The jury were told that the front door of the house led to a passage at the end where there was a stairway leading to the bedrooms. But Emily Ross stated that from her position in the bar area she would have seen anyone climbing those stairs and that no one had gone up or come down those stairs between 8 p.m. and 10 p.m., at which time she went out to look for her sister. Copestake, continuing with his evidence, now said that he had found his wife's body on the floor and that he pulled her away from under the bed. It was only then that he noticed the blood on her mouth and presumed that she had been sick. He told the jury that she had been drinking for five weeks now and had not eaten for nearly a month. Copestake said that she had fallen out of bed many times before and she had also fallen down the cellar steps. He estimated that she had fourteen or fifteen falls to his knowledge. This excuse, frequently given in cases of domestic violence, appeared not to move the coroner one jot. He called the surgeon back to the stand and asked him if, in his opinion, Mrs Copestake had not eaten for a month. Mr Dibbs stated that the body of the deceased appeared to be a well-fed woman who had a considerable amount of fat on her. There was no doubt in the jury's mind that Copestake was evading the responsibility of his actions by lying about the events as they had occurred.

The coroner summed up the evidence and the *Sheffield & Rotherham Independent* reported that he stated that:

> Someone had inflicted the bruises, but the jury must exhibit caution, as there was no direct evidence of who had done it, but there were just a few people in the house at the time of the assault. His mind was clear who had done it, but the jury had to make up their own minds. If they clearly thought that Copestake had inflicted the wound then they had a case of murder and he must go for trial. There was no case for manslaughter in it. If they were unsure that he had done it, then it would have to record an open verdict.

For confirmation he called Mr Dibbs back to the stand to clarify if he had examined Copestake's boots and if he was certain that they had caused the wound. The doctor agreed on both counts. Sergeant Bradbury stated that there was no sign of blood on the boots when the man had been arrested the following day. The jury only took fifteen minutes to record a verdict of willful murder, but apparently there had been some dissention in the ranks as only eleven out of twelve were in favour of the verdict. The coroner sent them back to deliberate for a further thirty minutes and a surprising verdict was given, considering the coroner's summing up, as one of manslaughter. There were still members of the jury who were not happy with the verdict, as a reporter of the local newspaper stated that, 'it was only fair to say that one or two members of the jury refused to sign the paper giving the verdict'. The coroner sentenced Copestake to be tried at the Leeds Assizes and dismissed the jury.

The contradiction in the given verdict was a matter of great dissention, and it did not end there. The following week one of the prosecution team, Mr Chambers, appeared before the Sheffield magistrates asking that the verdict be changed to one of willful murder rather than manslaughter. He stated that the woman had been found with badly swollen hands, as would have been expected in defence wounds. That, combined with the fact that the toe of Copestake's boot fitted into the injury very closely, inevitably pointed to his guilt in the case. The magistrate asked Mr Chambers if any fresh evidence had been brought forward and he had to admit that it hadn't. A date was put forward for the magistrates to discuss the matter on 28 August 1865, but they deliberated that with no further evidence that he be sent for trial for manslaughter.

Copestake appeared before the Leeds Assizes on Monday 9 December where he pleaded not guilty to the charge. He was questioned about why he had waited so long before getting a doctor to attend the injured woman. He said that on Thursday, when his wife was still insensible, he went to fetch Dr Booth who was not in. He returned to the lodging house and told Selina Kitson and she urged him to find another doctor. He then went to the surgery of Dr Skinner who, he was told, would not be back until 2 p.m. It was at this point that he suddenly asked Kitson, his wife and her sister to leave and not to come back any more. Copestake's defence team was led by Mr Waddy, who made a good case for his client, stating that the prisoner had found his wife lying on the floor on her back and she was insensible. He pointed out that as she was on her back he would not have seen the wound at the back of her head and that was why he was misled into thinking she had been drugged. Mr Waddy pointed out that Mrs Copestake had a history of drunkenness and that she had fallen out of bed on several occasions. He made the point that she could have fallen onto a utensil (which with Victorian sensibilities could only have been the chamber pot) that caused the injury. She had collected the takings and anyone in the house may have realized this and robbed her. He said that despite Emily Rose's statement to the contrary, it would not be difficult to distract a child while an accomplice went upstairs and that robbery could have been the motive for the crime. He minimized the importance of the bruising on the body of the deceased due to her drunkenness, but the witnesses had given evidence that there had been several incidents of domestic violence over the time the couple had been at the beerhouse. Despite the spirited way in which his defence argued the case, the jury returned after a very short while and gave the verdict that Copestake was guilty of manslaughter. When asked if he had anything to say, the prisoner replied that he was innocent, but it seems the judge was unmoved and sentenced him to sixteen years imprisonment.

The life of Elizabeth Copestake was short and brutal, but like everywhere else in Britain, a divorce was not an option for working class women. But the men of Sheffield were very resourceful when it came to ridding themselves of their wives in a way which did not include murder; this was the practice of wife selling. It was usual that the husband sold her to a friend or companion who would pay him an agreed amount. If the woman had been very badly treated or threatened she would agree to the sale and she would be sold in the market place, in some cases being exhibited with a halter over her head in the same way that cattle would be sold.

The local newspaper reported that crowds started gathering at the market place in Sheffield at noon on Tuesday 12 January 1847 to witness a wife sale which had been advertised around the town. What really appeared to upset the sensibilities of the residents was not the sale itself or the sad position of the woman, but the crowds of people obstructing the entrance to the market itself. Many of the crowd were standing on boxes and fences to have a better view. The young woman's name was Harriett Trotter and she had only been married to her husband Robert for a year. When the police arrived they found the husband had gone looking for the buyer, who was a workmate of his and they took the woman to the Town Hall, dispersing the crowd at the same time. A warrant was issued against the husband and the pair were brought before the magistrate the following day. She was described by a reporter as being a 'poor creature, an object of pity who was in great distress'. Trotter had treated her so badly that she had brought him before the bench a month previously and he was so incensed by this that he had threatened her with a pistol until that she had agreed to the sale. The magistrate castigated the man for the ill treatment of his wife and he was ordered to provide sureties to keep the peace for six months.

As we have seen, the lot of women was often not a happy one in the city of Sheffield, and they were often subject to the vagaries of men. Many took refuge in alcohol, which in turn led to fights and brawls, occasionally ending in murder. Some cases appear to be just unlucky, whilst others indicate a sadistic, cold-blooded and calculated ending of a person's life.

Chapter Eight

—◆—

A Disturbance in Market Street

As we have seen, in Sheffield fights could break out at any time. If they happened in a public house the brawl would often be taken outside in the pub yard to come to a conclusion which would not result in breaking the pub furniture or windows. Such a fight broke out on Tuesday April 23 1861 in the Cup Inn on Market Street between two men. This time, however, the consequences were longer lasting, resulting in a man's death.

An inquest was held on Thursday 25th before the deputy coroner, Mr J. Webster Esq., at the Town Hall on the body of Samuel Salt, aged twenty-three years. It seems that the deceased had been out drinking with a group of friends, including John Benns, from about 3 p.m. and at sometime between 6 p.m. and 7 p.m. they had decided that they were going to the Cup Inn in Market Street. They had only been in the pub about twenty minutes when Salt got into an altercation with his brother-in-law, George Allen, who said that he still owed him 9s 6d and stated that 'it was about time he paid up'. Salt told him that he had no money to pay him, but he would pay the debt when he had some. Allen, not content with this, called him a 'bad, unprincipled man'. Salt jumped up, tearing off his jacket, saying 'you can take it out of me if you want'. At this point, Charles Fletcher intervened and offered to fight Salt, who took off his coat to fight him, but as he was not sober his friends made him put his coat back on.

In the confusion that followed and due no doubt to the amount of alcohol consumed, a friend who worked with Salt, called Moore, offered to fight Fletcher on Salt's behalf, but he declined. To add to the confusion a man called Dakin offered to fight on Fletcher's behalf and he and Moore went outside in the yard to settle their differences. They were followed out by the rest of the men in the pub, approximately twelve in number, who were determined to watch the fight. One observer, Charles Thorpe, a waiter at the Cup Inn, stood by the door leading into the public house. He had tried to stop the men from fighting, but they were equally determined that it would go ahead. Thorpe stood about three yards from where the fight was taking place in the yard, which by now was grabbing the attention of the crowd, when, to his

The Town Hall with the extension containing the Magistrates' Court at the rear. (Chris Drinkall)

amazement, he saw Fletcher go behind Salt and hit him four times on the head, felling him to the ground. Thorpe told the inquest that there was no one in between himself and Salt and he had seen the whole occurrence. Salt had not seen Fletcher, who stood behind him to carry out the cowardly attack. No words had been spoken by either of the men and Salt was left senseless on the ground. The landlady, Mrs Whitworth, had sent for the police when the fight broke out. Thorpe ran up to the felled man and said to Fletcher that 'you shouldn't have hit a man from behind' but Fletcher was equally sure that he was shamming. By the time Police Constable William Pople arrived, it was obvious that Salt was dying.

A surgeon was called for and arrived shortly afterwards. The surgeon, Mr W.F. Fotherby, arrived to find Salt on the point of death and, in fact, he died shortly afterwards. He completed the post-mortem the following day and he told the coroner that Salt had extravasations of blood on the surface and base of the brain arising from a blow or a fall. There were contused wounds over the right eye and no other external marks of violence. He stated that death had been a result of these injuries. The coroner asked him if death could have been caused by the amount of alcohol which he had taken and the excitement stirred in his blood from the disturbance in the public house, but the surgeon said no. Death was a result of his injuries. The constable took Fletcher into custody but when he was charged he stated that 'he had never struck Salt'.

John Benns gave evidence that Salt was not sober when they went to the Cup Inn. In other pubs around the town he had consumed six lots of 2d worth of black beer and some rum. He had asked for a drink at the Cup Inn but had not touched it when the fight broke out. In the row with Allen, his brother-in-law said some very cruel things to him which distressed Salt and Benns described him as 'crying like child'. That was when his workmate, Moore, offered to defend his friend and he told Allen that 'you should not have used him so'. Salt had been the last person to go out to the yard to watch the men fight and he was still crying when Moore went outside. Benns was watching the fight and then all of a sudden he saw his friend on the floor. He did not witness the attack by Fletcher. He told the jury that he thought he had had a fit or something. Benns rushed to his friend's side and Fletcher told him to slap his face to bring him round as he still thought that Salt was shamming. Benns told the inquest that Fletcher was by now looking quite anxious as he began to realize the position he was in.

At this point in the inquest, the accounts appeared to differ from the previous witnesses. William Riley was present in the inn and he told the jury that Salt and his brother-in-law, Allen, had both been betting at the Doncaster races, and that Salt had been winning and did have some cash, although he denied it to Allen. He also stated that he did not see Fletcher hit Salt and, in fact, to do so would have been impossible as Salt had been stood against the wall at the time, so it would have been unfeasible for Fletcher to come up behind him. Robert Hawksworth of Earl Street said that he

Earl Street. (Reproduced courtesy of Picture Sheffield)

had been one of the men that Salt had wanted to fight in the pub. Congratulating him on his winnings at the racecourse, Hawksworth said to him, 'Well Sam thou has been lucky again', referring to his winnings. Salt seemed annoyed and Hawksworth said that he threatened to 'knock my neck out'. When Hawksworth asked him what was the matter he would not explain and instead took off his coat to fight him. Allen then came in and angry words were exchanged and, at this point, Salt became distressed. His friend, Moore, stated that 'he is my mate and I will not let him fight as he is drunk'. At this point, Dakin offered to fight Moore. His brother, George Hawksworth, also stated that Fletcher had not hit Salt, saying that he was looking at Salt when he fell as if in a fit. At this point, he said, the fight was over and Moore was back in the inn.

The coroner, irritated no doubt by the discrepancies, stated that he was of the opinion that the whole party should have been committed for manslaughter. The evidence from the surgeon gave the reason very clearly for death. The coroner stated that the only evidence that could be believed was given by the waiter, Thorpe, who was the most objective due to the fact that he was sober at the time. The other statements had been made by friends of either party and were therefore not to be relied on for accuracy. The coroner stated that he did not believe a word of the last witness. All the parties were drunk and he questioned whether landlords should let clients get into such a state of excitement that fighting was the only outcome. The jury consulted with each other for only fifteen minutes before returning a verdict of manslaughter against Charles Fletcher. The coroner sent him to be tried at the next York Assizes. Bail was given to Fletcher on two sureties of £50 each.

The trial at York Assizes on July 20 1861 was very much an anticlimax. The defence made a very good case that Samuel Salt died during a fit of apoplexy due to excitement and aggravated by alcohol. Fletcher was found not guilty and discharged. The victim was only twenty-three years old and we have no further knowledge about whether he was an alcoholic or had any other health problems that would have contributed to his death. But what cannot have been taken into consideration was the fact that Fletcher was determined to fight Salt for some unknown grievance. He challenged him to a fight almost as soon as he had entered the pub and was only deterred by the friends of Salt who felt that he was too drunk. When another man challenged Fletcher to fight on Salt's behalf, he declined. His cowardly attack on Salt, an unsuspecting victim, was surely proof that he wanted him dead, although we will never know the reason why.

The very different nature of the cases in this anthology of murder emphasise the fact that it can happen at anytime to anyone. Some are premeditated and some are murder by chance. But the most heinous crimes are those inflicted by a parent on very young children.

Chapter Nine

⟹◆⟸

'Don't hurt me, Father'

In January 1881 most of the population of Sheffield was talking about the Boer War which had started in South Africa and many Sheffield people volunteered to go out to fight. This was later to be known as the First Boer War and lasted for a year. The newspaper was full of the victories and the defeats of battle. In the next case, the uncle of the deceased had been fighting in South Africa and had returned home to find some peace and quiet away from the battles and to celebrate Christmas in his home town of Sheffield. Unfortunately, he was involved in a murder which happened within his own family.

The town of Sheffield was shocked on Monday 3 January 1881 when the facts of the following case were spread around the town. Charles Henry Sampson had been drinking steadily since before Christmas. Rather than celebration however, it caused him to develop delirium tremens resulting in the murder of his six-month-old daughter. He was a file forger employed at the works of Messrs Waterfall of Bailey Lane. He was twenty-six years of age and had been married for eight years, resulting in five children. He lived with his wife in one of the many courtyards of the town, which were so numerous that the authorities numbered them rather than give them a name. He lived at No. 4 House, No. 4 Court on Cumberland Street. He was described as 'not a steady man' who had not been eating whilst steadily drinking. On Friday 31 December he began to shown such signs of agitation and excitement that his wife became so alarmed that she was glad that her brother, John Owen, who was on leave from his regiment, was staying at the house. Along with the parents and the children was her father-in-law, who shared the attic bedroom in one bed with four of the children in the other. Her brother-in-law, Edward Exley, also lived not too far away in West Street.

All day Friday he appeared like a wild man and Mrs Sampson was afraid to go to bed with him. She called for Dr Thompson to come and see him and try to calm him down. Instead of giving him some medication to calm him, he told her that she must not leave him on his own as he was a danger to himself and may jump out of

A Sheffield soldier during the Boer War. (Reproduced courtesy of Picture Sheffield)

the bedroom window or he might injure someone. He urged her to go and see Dr Willingham and ask that he give her a ticket for the workhouse where he could be contained in the padded cell there and looked after properly. On Saturday he appeared to be no better and, as a consequence, Owen took him for a walk. He had a couple of drinks and returned to the house about lunchtime when he was persuaded to have a sleep on the sofa for a few hours before waking at six o'clock. Later he wanted his wife to go to bed with him, but she was afraid to. She asked Owen to sleep with him that night as she was afraid. He complied, but he told his sister the next morning that Sampson kept gripping him wildly for most of the night and he had been unable to get much sleep. Sampson appeared to worsen as the day went on, attacking Owen and throwing him out of the house. Mrs Sampson left the house with the children and stayed with a neighbour in Jessop Street.

Inevitably, she was forced to return and with much trepidation the couple retired to bed. Her husband was shouting out so much that she got up about 3 a.m. and went downstairs. He followed her in just his shirt and she persuaded him to go back upstairs and put on some trousers. She carried the youngest child, Ruth, who had been in the same bed as the couple downstairs and making up a bed in the clothes basket, set it before the fire. At 6 a.m. he asked his wife to get him some brandy and water and, thinking that it may calm him, she agreed. When she went out into the court to the little shop there, she told some workmen that her husband was in a terrible state and asked them to intervene if there was any sign of trouble, which they agreed to do. She left her brother in the house to try to keep him calm. Obtaining the brandy, she returned to find that Owen had been attacked once again and was outside of the house. Hearing a scream and a dull thud, she realized that little Ruth was still in the house and she became very fearful for her safety. It later appeared that Sampson had picked her up by her feet and smashed her head against the hearthstone. He then proceeded with his fists to smash every pane of glass in the house. The shards of glass cutting into him resulted in blood running down his arms and injuring his feet. He smashed all the glass in the kitchen and the parlour and finally dashed up to the bedroom containing two beds, one occupied by his father and the other containing his four children. As he appeared in the doorway, looking wild with blood on his hands and feet, the eldest child, a boy called George William Sampson, aged eleven, looked at his father and said, 'Don't hurt me, father'. Sampson replied, 'I wont, love', and then smashed all the windows in the attic. Having accomplished this he ran downstairs and George shouted to ask if he could come downstairs. Sampson agreed and the boy went down the stairs where he saw his sister on the floor and went to pick her up. Before he did, he saw that her head was all smashed in and backed away. By now his father had jumped out of the kitchen window and ran away before anyone could stop him. George calmly took the other children to a neighbour's house.

Mrs Sampson had gone to the house of Dr Willingham in order to get her husband sent to the workhouse, but the servant told her that he was not there. Furthermore, he was never at the house on a Sunday as he had a country residence. Mrs Sampson told her that her husband was insane and she feared for the life of herself and the children, but the servant was unable to help as she pointed out there was no one in the house to send for the doctor. She then saw a constable and asked him to help her, but he was unable to help. Returning back to the house she found the body of her youngest child. One of the neighbours went to fetch constable Bestwick and he reported the murder to his superior officers at the Town Hall. Other constables were asked to look out for Sampson as it was thought that he was intent on killing himself. He was finally spotted in Milk Street about 6.45 a.m. and later about 7 a.m. in Sheaf Street by Constable Dye. As he spotted him, dressed only in a shirt and trousers, another constable, Charles Thompson, came up and they agreed to try to get the man into a cab and remove him to the workhouse. He was acting very bizarrely and pointing to the sky, but not speaking or answering the two policemen when they spoke to him. They managed to get him to a weigh house near to Park Station and called a cab. They had the utmost difficulty getting the man into the cab, not just because of his violent behaviour, but also because he was shaking with cold. When they arrived at the workhouse, the two officers helped the staff to put him into the padded cell. Sampson asked them not to put him in there as the room was on fire. He also said to Constable Thompson, 'I have murdered my child by dashing its head on the floor. If you go you will see'.

The workhouse doctor was called to see him shortly after his admittance at 8 a.m. and found him depressed through drink. He attended to his cuts, but due to his wild behaviour Sampson stayed at the workhouse for another three days. He had two guards assigned to watch him and the guard was changed every four hours. In the

Cumberland Street during demolition, showing a doorway leading into courtyard behind. (Reproduced courtesy of Picture Sheffield)

meantime, an inquest was held on his daughter at the Globe Inn on Jessop Street on Monday 5 January 1881. The news of the death had spread throughout the town and as a consequence the street outside the public house was full of people. The coroner, Mr Wightman, told the jury that Mr Sampson was unable to attend the inquest and he would adjourn until he could be present to the following Tuesday. On Wednesday 6 January he was calm enough to be handed over to the police and he was charged with the willful murder of Ruth Sampson, although he appeared to take little interest in the proceedings. He was remanded for a week so that he was able to attend the inquest, where he had a solicitor called Mr H. Knowle Binns.

The adjourned inquest was resumed on Tuesday 12 January 1881. Mr Arthur Hallam, the surgeon to the Sheffield police, appeared and described the child's injuries. The skull was extensively fractured and there were lacerations of the brain. The bones in the head at that age are very soft and so they would have given way readily. There were contusions on both sides of the chest where someone had grabbed the child violently. The coroner asked if the injuries to the head could have been caused if a large object such as a table had fallen on the baby, but Mr Hallam felt not as the head had been reduced to pulp and he felt that the child had been dashed against a hard substance two, or possibly three, times. The workhouse doctor, Mr Lewis Hunt, told the jury that Sampson had been admitted suffering from delirium tremens on the first day, but the following day he was better, although still wild and excitable. He told the coroner and the jury that he had no doubt that this had been caused by excessive drinking.

The coroner asked him if he could deduce the state of his mind at the time of the murder, but Mr Hunt told him that it was impossible to say. The delirium tremens affected people in different ways, making them fearful or paranoid.

Mrs Sampson's brother was the next to give his evidence. John Owen, a private in the 1st Battalion 24th Regiment who had been in South Africa, stated that on Saturday 1 January Sampson got up about 3 a.m. and he persuaded him to go back to sleep. He was woken at 6 a.m. by Sampson leaping on his bed and towering over him. Owen managed to pin him to the bed, but he was 'talking very queerly and acting wild'. When they both went downstairs, Sampson asked his wife if she would get him some rum and water and she did. He calmed down to such an extent that they went to the pub together. On the Saturday they went to Dr Thompson's house and he told them that a small port would probably be beneficial to him, so they went to the pub again. On the Sunday he woke about six o'clock to find Sampson dancing around the house saying that he could feel fire burning him and talking about Mother Shipton (an old woman of Knaresborough, North Yorkshire). He attacked Owen and threw him out of the house and he left to try to catch his sister returning with the brandy.

The mother of the deceased child appeared next and she told them that her husband had been drinking steadily over the Christmas period. On the Sunday he had asked her for some brandy and she had gone to get some as soon as it was light. When she returned, her brother met her saying that Sampson was quite mad. They heard him smashing all the windows and then he leapt out of the kitchen window and dashed

West Street as it looks today. (Chris Drinkall)

Above The Globe Inn, Jessop Street. (Reporduced courtesy of Picture Sheffield)
Below Jessop Street as it looks today. (Chris Drinkall)

out of the yard. That was when she went into the house and found out what had happened to the baby.

The coroner summed up the case for the jury and reminded them that there had been no witness to the crime, but the jury would be in little doubt as to how the deceased came to her death. However, the jury must come to the conclusion about his state of mind at the time of the murder. Suffering from delirium tremens was no defence in the eyes of the law. After a very short break, the jury stated that Charles Henry Sampson had committed willful murder on his daughter. They also asked that some censure be put on the parties who refused to get Sampson into the workhouse sooner, where he might have been prevented from committing the crime in which he was charged. Sampson was sent to the next session of the Leeds Assizes.

The trial of Sampson was heard on 5 February 1881 at the Stipendiary Court in Sheffield, where much was discussed about the state of his mind at the time of the murder. The judge, in directing the jury, stated that if they felt that Sampson was suffering from delirium tremens at the time of the murder and that as a consequence of which he did not know right from wrong, then he was not an accountable being. He cautioned them that, 'It will be your duty to acquit him on the grounds of insanity. But if you think from the evidence he did know what he was doing then you should offer a verdict of guilty of murder'.

After a few minutes deliberation, the jury found him not guilty on grounds of insanity. The judge ordered that the man be detained at Her Majesty's pleasure, stating that he hoped that 'if this case does not teach men the consequences of drink then nothing will'. Then Sampson was led sobbing very bitterly from the dock.

Chapter Ten

<hr/>

Quack Medicine

As we have seen there were parts of Sheffield, as with any city in the middle of the rapid industrial expansion, where it was positively dangerous to live. A complaint made by a solicitor of the town in March 1881, in a letter which was sent to the editor of the *Sheffield & Rotherham Independent*, stated:

> Sir,
> I think that attention of the Corporation and the members for St Peter's Ward attention should be drawn to the present state of the district below Bank Street and West Bar with a view of some improvement being effected. The houses are very dilapidated and inhabited by some very curious people. The district is giving the police some trouble. A Sergeant of Police and two constables are stationed there daily in The Waggon yard to prevent noisy disturbances in the locality which must be very expensive to the authorities and surely it is a thing which is not required and would not be if the inhabitants were improved off the ground.
> Yours truly,
> R. Knowles Binns.

For many people in the city living in such streets and courtyards, there was no proper sanitation and the water was tainted and unclean. Illness was rife and yet the very poor did not have money for proper health services. Medicine as we know it today was not available and they would be forced to buy 'medicine' from people who claimed to have far more medical knowledge than they actually had, who could offer potions for most ailments. The lives of children could be very precarious in the Victorian period and many homemade remedies would be used to help children sleep.

An inquest illustrating the problems parents had was held before the coroner, Mr T. Badger, on the body of John Norton, aged eleven months, at the White Hart at Oughtibridge in December 1847. The child had been in good health until its mother gave it some anodyne mixture made by a local woman named Mary Brookes. Anodyne was a medicine used for the relief of pain. It was a remedy which she had used on

ing Surgeons
...on. and 44, A...
...ce Engravings,
...atise on Syph-
...ing forms, in-
...of Gonorrhœa,
...deleterious In-
...rance of the
...and Body; to
...us on Debility,
...its attendant
...sidered, with
...by explanatory
...or the perfect
...from entering
...l consequences
...tion.
...inclosed with
...ille, (Price 2s.
...rdial Balm of
...) and is point-
...Friend, to be
...red confidence

...PILLS, Price
...nown through-
...st certain and
...age and symp-
...of time, con-
...y have effected
...ent and severe
...ms have failed;
...these Pills for
...tly contracted
...on is generally
...ularly recom-
...into the matri-
...parent are the
...his existence,
...offspring, with
..., and a variety
...introduced by

...sts, and Patent
...throughout the
...and America,
...the signature,
...expect. when
...e Pound, with-
...n of the com-
...are requested
...of their cases.
...M (Price 11s.
...those Persons
...their passions,
...eir way to the
...e affected with
...y its approach,
...stem, obstinate
...s, weaknesses,
...5 cases may be
...ents, which is

...PILLS, price
...out Europe for
..., and for Lues
...s in recent as

...d by Letter,
...o notice what-
...(postage pre-
...ute as possible

...be consulted as
...oors from Easy
..., Leeds. Only
...ntry patient, to
...k advice as will
...l effectual cure,
...al.

..., Patent Medi-
...er, can be sup-
...g Specific Pills,
...ual allowance
...holesale Patent

(No. 4.)

dren; for if a Child wakes in the ... young chil-
the Gums, the Syrup immediately gives ease; thereby
preventing Convulsions, Fevers, &c.—The great success
of this Medicine during the last Twenty-five Years has
induced unprincipled persons to imitate it, under the
name of American Soothing Syrup, and copying parts of
Mrs. Johnson's Bills, &c. Parents will, therefore be very
particular to ask for JOHNSON'S AMERICAN
SOOTHING SYRUP, and to notice that the names of
BARCLAY and SONS, 95 Farringdon Street, London, (to
whom Mrs. Johnson has sold the recipe,) are on the Stamp
affixed to each Bottle.—Sold by LEADER, Independent
Office, Sheffield.

MEDICAL ADVICE,
NO. 19, FIG-TREE LANE,
4 Doors from Bank street, Sheffield.

MR. SCOTT, Surgeon, who, after an extensive practice
of twenty-seven years, has rendered his counsel an
object of the utmost importance to all who are labouring
under the following complaints:—Bilious Disorders,
Giddiness in the Head, Deafness and Diseases of the Ear,
Rheumatism and Gout, Scrofula, Worms, Epileptic Fits,
Gravel. And to those who are troubled with Consump-
tion and Asthma, his Advice will be found invaluable.
Thousands have owned his skill. To the Youth of both
sexes, whether lured from health by the promptings of
passions, or the delusions of inexperience, his advice is
superior to all others in his practice. Where an early
application in a certain disorder, frequently contracted in
a moment of inebriety, he unites a mild gentleness of
treatment; the eradication is generally completed in a
few days, without restraint in diet, or hindrance of business, and insures the patient a permanent cure.
Patients from the country can be treated successfully
on describing minutely their case, and enclosing a remit-
tance for Advice and Medicine.
Mr. Scott, Surgeon, may be consulted daily as above.
☞ The Itch cured in One Hour.
19, Figtree lane, Four Doors from Bank street.
Surgery Two Doors above.

NEW COUGH MEDICINE.

HOLLAND'S BAL-
SAM of SPRUCE,
the newly discovered
remedy for COUGHS,
COLDS, INFLUENZA,
INCIPIENT ASTH-
MA, and CONSUMP-
TION.
Medical Science is daily
producing new wonders,
and among the discove-
ries which take place none are more deserving of public
approbation than a remedy for those complaints which, in
this variable climate, are so productive of fatal consequences to the comfort and lives of the public as COUGHS
and COLDS.
THIS EXTRAORDINARY REMEDY relieves the
most distressing symptoms in a few hours, and a little per-
severance in its use will, in every case, effect a permanent
cure.
COUGHS AND COLDS, accompanied with a difficulty
of breathing, soreness and rawness of the chest, impeded
expectoration, sore throat, and feverish symptoms, will be
quickly subdued, while its use will assuredly prevent con-
sumption from this prolific cause.
HOLLAND'S BALSAM OF SPRUCE gives imme-
diate ease in all Asthmatic cases, and particularly in
Hoarseness, Wheezings and Obstructions of the Chest;
while those who have laboured for years under the misery
of a confirmed Asthma, have been enabled by its use to
enjoy the blessings of life, and to pursue their avocations
with a degree of ease and comfort they had been strangers
to for years.
Prepared by Charles Holland, and sold by his agent,
WILLIAM HALLETT, 83, High Holborn, London, by all
the Wholesale Houses, and by at least one person in every
town in the Kingdom. Price, 1s. 1½d. per Bottle.
Sold also by the following respectable Agents:—
LEADER, Whitaker, Sheffield; Atkinson, Chesterfield;
Brooke and Co., Doncaster; Cardwell, Wakefield; Sis-
sons, Worksop; Gething, Mansfield; Whitham, Ash-
bourne; Wright, Macclesfield; Spivy, Huddersfield.

A WHITE POWDER of Oriental Herbs of the most
delightful fragrance.—It eradicates Tartar and decayed
Spots from the Teeth, preserves the Enamel, and fixes
the Teeth firmly in their sockets, rendering them deli-
cately white. Being an Anti-Scorbutic, it eradicates the
Scurvy from the Gums, strengthens, braces, and renders
them of a healthy red; it removes unpleasant tastes from
the mouth, which often remain after fevers, taking medi-
cine, &c., and imparts a delightful fragrance to the breath.
Price 2s. 9d. per Box, duty included.
NOTICE.—The Name and Address of the Proprietors.
A. ROWLAND & SON, 20 HATTON GARDEN,
LONDON,
Are engraved on the Government Stamp, which is pasted
on the two latter Articles; also printed, in red, on the
Wrapper in which each is enclosed.
Many SHOPKEEPERS offer for sale Counterfeits of the
above, composed of the most pernicious ingredients.
They call their trash the "GENUINE," and sign A. Row-
land Son, omitting the "&," recommending them as be-
ing cheap.
Be sure to ask for "ROWLAND'S."
Sold by them, and by respectable PERFUMERS and MEDI-
CINE VENDERS.

TO LADIES.

THE ONLY GENUINE WIDOW WELCH'S
PILLS are those prepared by Mrs. SMITHERS,
(Grand daughter to the Widow WELCH,) from the real
Family Recipe, without the least variation whatever.
This Medicine is justly celebrated for all Female Complaints, Nervous Disorders, Weakness of the Solids, Loss
of Appetite, Sick Head Ache, Lowness of Spirits, and
particularly for irregularities in the Female System. Mrs.
Smithers recommends Mothers, Guardians, Managers of
Schools, and all those who have the care of Females at an
early age, never to be without this useful Medicine.
The following is a recent and unsolicited testimonial to
their good effects.
10th August, 1839.—Dear Madam,—Obligation and
gratitude compel me to acknowledge the benefit that, with
God's blessing, three boxes of your Widow Welch's Pills
have been to my daughter, Mary Raynsford, seventeen
years of age, all hopes being ready to expire relative to
her recovery; her illness was occasioned from taking cold,
from being wet three years ago in the Hop Gardens, which
terminated in the dropsy, and extreme weakness, and
shortness of breath; but after taking three boxes of your
more than valuable Pills, she is quite restored to health.
I am, Madam, yours most respectfully,
JAMES RAYNSFORD.
Red Pale House, Dallington, Sussex.
IMPORTANT CAUTION.—The medicine sold in the
name of Kearsley, for the Widow Welch's Pills, is not
the genuine; and as the public are greatly deceived by the
advertisements put forth, Mrs. SMITHERS, the ONLY
REAL PROPRIETOR and Possessor of the Recipe,
Grand-daughter of the late Widow Welch, feels it her
duty, not only in defence of her own and SOLE RIGHT, but
as a protection to the public against every imposition, to
declare HERSELF the ONLY PERSON entitled to the
Original Recipe, or at all authorised to make or prepare
the said Medicine. To put the fact beyond all doubt, and
more fully to expose the conduct of persons who endea-
vour to deprive her of her right, the reader is referred to
the following AFFIDAVIT:—First—That she is in possession of the ONLY original and genuine Family Recipe.
...Second—That this Recipe was handed down by the
Widow Welch to her aunts Mary and Sarah Welch, and
by them to her; and that these Pills are prepared by her
from the real Family Recipe, without the least variation
whatever.....Third—That she prepared them from her
aunts Mary and Sarah Welch, before they were known or
sold by Mr. Kearsley; her aunts being infirm through age
and sickness, rendered them incapable of preparing them.
Sworn before WILLIAM CURTIS, Lord Mayor.
February 18, 1796.
Observe, that the genuine are wrapped in blue paper,
and signed on the label by Mrs. Smithers. Price 2s. 9d.
per box. Sold by LEADER, Radley, Lofthouse, Slack,
Whitaker, Smith, Newton, Ridge and Jackson, She...
Harrison, Wall, Pybus, Ray, Barnsley; D...
well, Gell, Hurst, Lawton, Mountain, Shee...
field, Marsden, Knowles, Wakefield; Bri...
Priestley, Pontefract; Rhodes, Snaith; W...
Brooke and Co., Hopper, Hartley, Donc...
most Druggists and Medicine Vendors.

Patent medicine and medical advice on offer in Sheffield newspapers. Note the proud boast of Mr Scott, surgeon, 'Itch cured in one hour'. (*Sheffield & Rotherham Independent*, 13 November 1841)

The White Hart at Oughtibridge. (Reproduced courtesy of Picture Sheffield)

her own children and consisted of a compound of opium, treacle and Spanish juice boiled with water. The mother gave some of the mixture to her son on Wednesday and he immediately went to sleep and never woke up, dying the following day. The coroner castigated the mother and Mary Brookes for giving the child medicine which contained opium, but the jury brought in a verdict of 'overdose of anodyne administered without any intention of injuring it'.

The people who sold these kinds of preparations were known as 'quacks' and for centuries had sold their wares in markets and fairs, whilst others had use of business premises. Advertisements for medicine for coughs, widow's complaints and medical advice proliferated in the local newspapers of the time. People professing to be herbalists and medical botanists sold remedies for just a few pennies, but sometimes the need would be more sinister. Two of these Sheffield herbalists in 1881 were approached by a young woman seeking an abortion.

Alice Fleet Smith was twenty-one years of age and in March 1881 she lived at her father's house in Hemmingfield, near Barnsley. She was the eldest of five children and had been 'courting' Tom Turner, a grocer's assistant of Elsecar, for almost six years and they were planning soon to marry. At first her father hadn't approved of Turner, but was gradually coming to like him since they announced their engagement. Turner was a steady and reliable young man who for the last year had been in the habit of giving her 10s a week towards the couple being able to set up home together. The only blot on this idyllic landscape was when Alice found that she was pregnant. She talked

Shops on Division Street on the site of Mrs Mary Dover's surgical instrument shop. (Chris Drinkall)

about it to Turner, telling him that she did not want 'to get married in disgrace' and declared that she was going to get rid of it. She had heard of a man in Sheffield who was a herbalist who could give her something to cause an abortion and in February 1881 went to see him. His name was Mr Simmonite and he was a medical botanist occupying two rooms in Thomas Street, Sheffield. Turner accompanied her, although the consultation, lasting twenty-five minutes, took place with Smith and Simmonite in another room. He gave her some medicine which she took, but it did not have the desired effect.

Smith went back later having borrowed £2 from her father and asked him for something a bit stronger as the potion had been unsuccessful. At first he said that he couldn't help her, but no doubt due to her desperate plight he sent her along to Mrs Mary Dover who had a surgical instrument shop in Division Street, Sheffield. On 31 January 1881, Smith went into the shop. What transpired was a mystery that was never revealed, but when she left the shop she became very ill. She got as far as the Sheffield station and found herself in a lot of pain. Mrs Dover had told her that 'no matter how painful it is you will be alright'. By the time she got home she wanted nothing but her bed. Mrs Dover had told her that she was not to call the doctor in until after the foetus had been expelled because after that 'no doctor in the world can tell when it is over'. Dover had warned her that it would be painful, but she had no idea that it would be as bad as it was. Arriving home she went straight to bed. When Turner came around to see her, he was very concerned about the amount of pain she was in. So much so that he went to see Mrs Dover to ask her what kind of instrument she had used and he asked her, 'Had it been sharp?' Mrs Dover showed him a speculum, a round-ended tool which had been used from Roman times to investigate body cavities, particularly the vagina. She told him that 'she had helped many a dozen [women] and have never had a mishap yet'. Impressing on him again that there would be some pain, she sent him away. On 4 February when he visited Smith once again, she showed him a clot of blood the size of an egg which had been expelled from her body during the night.

By this time her father, Edward Smith, was very concerned about her as she had been in bed since the night of 31 January. He had returned home from work at seven o'clock to find her in great pain. She would not allow him to go for a doctor and only left her bed to have fresh sheets put on it. Finally, by 8 February, a doctor was called to see her. Mr William Ritchie, a surgeon of Hoyland, called on her and attended her twice a day. By the 12 February he realized that her condition was a critical one and told her that she would have to make a deposition. These dying depositions were critical as when the patient was about to die it was felt that they were bound to tell the truth, giving greater emphasis to magistrates and jury members. He took down her statement and she described the abortion to him. She told him that Mrs Dover had charged her two guineas. The girl died on 21 February after enduring almost three weeks of pain.

Mrs Mary Dover was arrested at her shop in Division Street and charged with the willful murder of Alice Fleet Smith. The inquest was held at the Barnsley Police Court and Mrs Dover, who had no solicitor, was found guilty and sent to appear before the magistrates on Tuesday 1 March. The court was crowded with spectators all clamouring to see the abortionist who had caused the death of the young girl. Mrs Dover appeared dressed all in black and by now she had secured the services of Mr Fairburn, a solicitor of Sheffield. She was allowed to have a seat at the solicitors' table and it was reported that she took a great interest in the proceedings. For many years she had provided similar operations for many local women. Dr Ritchie undertook the post-mortem with Dr Blackburn and found three distinct punctures on the usuteri. He was asked if the injuries could be caused by the catheter found on Mrs Dover's premises and he agreed that it could have been the instrument used. Catheters were now being used by Victorian abortionists as safer than the syringe method previously used. The operation involved opening up the cervix with an instrument such as a speculum and inserting the catheter to irritate the uterus, resulting in the foetus being expelled. Dr Ritchie said that the primary cause of Smith's death was the abortion and the secondary cause of death was peritonitis and blood poisoning. The defence solicitor made very little effort to save his client stating that, 'After hearing all the evidence their worships could only consider a prima facie case and it would therefore be useless to make a case for the defence'. The jury took only moments to find her guilty and the magistrate signed the order for her to be sent to the Assizes. Mr Fairborn requested that she be released on bail until her trial, but the magistrates would not allow this due to the seriousness of the crime.

By the time that Dover came to trial, it had been decided that the more serious crime of murder be dropped and that she be tried on the lesser charge of procuring an abortion. The defence, Mr Digby Seymour QC, stated that there was no doubt that the death of a young girl had resulted by her own actions, although she had not intended for it to happen. Nevertheless the act was unlawful and therefore she was responsible for it. She had already pleaded guilty to the charge of using instruments to facilitate an abortion by mechanical means. He asked his Lordship to show as much leniency as he could to the prisoner who was a widow with three young children to maintain and had repented sincerely for her conduct. The judge asked if she had been in trouble before and was told that she hadn't. The jury returned a verdict of guilty to the lesser charge and she was sentenced to penal servitude for five years.

No doubt Mrs Dover lived to regret what had happened to Alice Fleet Smith and no doubt there were many more of her ilk who would provide these services in and around the town. Only with the legalization of abortion in 1967 could women have this operation performed safely. Perhaps she was just an ignorant woman, as very little was known about germs and the need to sterilize instruments. Although Joseph Lister had written a paper on the needs to sterilize instruments and use carbolic soap during medical operations in September 1867, such information would not have been readily available to a woman working in surgical instrument shop.

Mrs Dover was clearly not a malicious woman but the next case indicates a young man who was truly evil and heartless in his desire to rob and almost kill a defenceless old man who had shown him nothing but kindness.

Chapter Eleven

———◆◆◆———

A Thoroughly Bad Sort

There have always been people prepared to rob others rather than get steady, respectable employment for themselves, and sometimes the wrong person was arrested for the crime. One such robbery took place on 25 March 1861 and later that same day James McCabe was charged with stealing three gold watches, the property of Messrs Burrell & Co., Sheffield. It was alleged that he went into the shop and asked to look at all three watches and, seizing his opportunity, grabbed them from the counter and ran out the shop with them. James McCabe had been seen near to the shop and shortly afterwards he was arrested. His alibi was that he had been in his brother, Thomas McCabe's, company. Other witnesses swore not only to his good character but that he was in Sussex Street at the time of the robbery. The judge, summing up, pointed out to the jury the good character he was known for up to now and the many discrepancies of the witnesses statements. He recommended that the jury find him not guilty and McCabe was discharged.

Other disreputable types however entered into the crime of robbery in a much more brutal fashion. Ralph Barber was seventy-eight years of age, retired, and had been enjoying his retirement very much. He had spent most of his life as a joiner's tool maker and had made enough money to manage his retirement quite well. He lived in a detached house on Brook Street, Brook Hill, which was in its own yard with a high wall all the way around it preserving his privacy. He was reported to have an aversion to strangers and since his housekeeper left him to marry, he had engaged the services of a woman called Mrs Mason, who came in to cook and clean for him every day. He had been described as an eccentric but kindly man and he was generous to a fault. On Saturday 4 May 1861, about five o'clock, he was pottering around in his kitchen when someone knocked on the kitchen door. He opened the door slightly to find himself confronted by a young man who had been to his house once before. The young man was Samuel Mitchell, aged nineteen, and he had come to his house three weeks previously asking if the housekeeper, Mrs Mason, was in. Barber told him that she wasn't and he had said that his mother (Mrs Mason's sister) had wanted to ask Mrs Mason to borrow a sovereign from Barber to help her in her greengrocer's shop.

An account of the attempted murder by Samuel Mitchell. (*Sheffield & Rotherham Independent*, 13 July 1861)

A sovereign, a coin which went out of circulation by 1914, was the equivalent to a pound. Barber immediately put his hand in his pocket saying, 'If that's all I can lend you, a sovereign' and without hesitation gave him the money.

The truth came out when Barber mentioned it to his housekeeper, who spoke to her sister and realized that Mitchell had lied to the old man to gain money through false pretences. Mitchell's older brother, William, who was known as a reliable and respectable man, went to see Mr Barber to apologize and to offer to pay the old man out of his own pocket as soon as he heard what his brother had done. Barber told him that he appreciated the offer and suggested that as times were bad and trade was not good that they split the difference and he pay him back a half a sovereign, to which he agreed. Apologizing once more for the fraud which his brother Samuel had committed, William paid him the money and left. The old man thought that was that and was therefore very surprised to see Mitchell turn up once more at his door.

The young man pushed his way into the house and Barber asked him what he wanted. Mitchell became very contrite and asked Mr Barber to forgive him for taking money under false pretences. Barber told him that his brother had been to see him and as far as he was concerned the case was closed, but Mitchell still showed no inclination to leave. The old man again asked him what he wanted and he said that he had been thinking about what had happened and he wanted to get down on his knees to apologize to Mr Barber. By now, Barber was getting anxious and he told him that there was no need, but Mitchell got down on his knees and asked the old man to forgive him. Barber leaned towards him to lift him up off his knees when Mitchell savagely attacked him, beating him around the head with his fists. Grabbing a poker from the nearby fireplace he proceeded to hit him over the head with that. Barber realized that his long drawn out act of contrition was just a ruse to find out if anyone else was in the house. He was hitting him so hard that blood was pouring from Barber's head and streaming down the walls. Eventually he pushed the old man up stairs. Mr Barber had difficulty climbing the stairs and Mitchell was almost carrying him by the time they reached the top. Laying the old man on his bed, Mitchell threatened 'to finish him off' and then told him to turn out his pockets, which contained 2s 6d and the key to his desk. In the desk was the key to the safe in which he kept all his valuables, which was hidden in a cupboard in his bedroom. Mitchell didn't see it and just rifled through the desk drawers which were not locked. Finally looking around to see if there were any more valuable objects, Mitchell left the room. Hearing the door close a short time later, Barber managed to get downstairs and raise the alarm. He opened one of the sash windows from the parlour and shouted for help as loud as he could.

His neighbour from next door, Mr William Short, had witnessed a young man running down the passage on to the street in front of Barber's house about 5.20 p.m. Within a few minutes he heard Barber's cries and ran to help the old man. When he went into the house the neighbour found the old man in a dreadful state. There was blood pouring from his head and blood on his face and hands. He had several bruises on his head and arms that were inflicted when he was trying to defend himself. His face and neck was badly bruised, the bruising on the neck being consistent with the old man being grasped around the throat. A surgeon, Mr Henry George Allenson, was called and he found Barber sitting up in a chair being cared for by his neighbour and his wife. Examining the wounds on his head, he found that the injury had gone so deep that the bones of the skull had been exposed. He arranged for Barber to go to bed and helped the old man up the stairs to make him comfortable in his own bed. He then sent a message to the magistrate, Mr J. Jobson Smith, who in turn gave the information to the chief constable, Mr Jackson, who sent a constable to arrest Mitchell. Detective

Officer Richard Brayshaw attended the house shortly afterwards. He asked the old man to give a statement which he wrote down. He told the officer that Mitchell had smelt of liquor when he came into the house and described how he had lingered to make sure that no one else was about. Brayshaw removed from the house a tea tray, the poker and some newspapers all covered in blood. He was almost back at the Town Hall when he was met by the two Mitchell brothers. It seems that Mitchell had gone to a pub and returned back to his home where he found his brother waiting for him. William had heard what his brother had done and was taking him to the Town Hall to give himself up. Brayshaw took him into custody. Mitchell was drunk and still had spots of blood on the front of his shirt. Examining his pockets, the officer found a handkerchief with blood on it and he reported that the blood was still wet. Brayshaw then took Mitchell back to Barber's house to confront his victim and to hear Mr Barber's signed statement. Whilst at the house a piece of cloth was found on the hearthstone which matched the material of the coat that Mitchell was still wearing.

Mitchell was brought into the Town Hall on Thursday before the magistrate, Mr J. Jobson Smith. The surgeon, Mr Allenson, gave a list of the old man's injuries which included several contusions on his head caused by a blunt instrument, the skull being clearly seen. The surgeon had considered the old man to be in grave danger due to his age and his injuries and as a consequence of which he had visited every day. The magistrate asked him if he considered the old man still to be in danger and he replied that he was. On examining him that morning he had found matter under a wound which he feared might prove fatal. The magistrate then insisted that Mitchell, who had still been drunk the last time he was escorted to Barber's house, be taken there again now sober. Following this the prisoner was asked if there was anything he wanted to say. He stated that, 'I'll never do another such crime while I live. I was rather silly [drunk] when I did it. I hope that Mr Barber will get over it and forgive me this time. That's all I have to say'. The magistrate then told him that he was to be sent to be tried at the Assizes on a charge of 'cutting and wounding with intent feloniously, wilfully and of malice aforethought to kill and murder Ralph Barber'.

Samuel Mitchell was taken to trial before Baron Martin on 13 July 1861. At the trial Barber's statement was read out as he was still in a weak state and unable to attend. Dr Allenson was still attending him on a regular basis. The evidence of Mitchell lingering at the house was discussed and extreme poverty was offered as a reason for the crime. But the jury was unmoved as they gave a verdict of wounding with intent to do grievous bodily harm. The sentence given to Mitchell was that he be imprisoned for eighteen months.

The viciousness with which Mitchell attacked Mr Barber was thought to be an attempt to murder the old man and why he spared his life was never discussed or fully understood. Maybe he repented at the last moment or did not have the bottle to go though with it. We shall never know. The next case took more planning and thought but nevertheless was an attempt to deprive someone of their life.

Chapter Twelve

―――◆―――

White Powder in the Beer

A crime which is relatively unknown today took place in Victorian Sheffield in July of 1861; the 'breach of promise'. A woman of 'rather above forty years of age', Elizabeth Thompson, was pledged to marry a young man of twenty-five years, Edwin Outhwaite. She was the owner of a lodging house in Sheffield and he went to live with her there. Relations between the couple were strained when, whilst still unmarried, she gave birth to a baby that unfortunately died at birth. Outhwaite had agreed that he would marry her but as they were second cousins he stated that he would prefer to wait until his father had died, the reason given was that the relationship between the couple was within prohibited degrees. When his father died in 1860, he bequeathed several thousands of pounds to his second wife. Outhwaite knew that he was due to inherit some of this money on his stepmother's death. Subsequently the banns were called but Outhwaite, having cooled off somewhat, neglected to keep his promise. The judge found the case proven and awarded Miss Thompson damages of £80.

It seems that women who owned a lodging house were viewed as being an asset to any young man seeking a fortune and the following case illustrates the desirability of a well-off widow owning property and a shop and the lengths a man would go to possess such a woman. Widow Sarah Liversedge let out rooms of her house in Eyre Street to lodgers. At sometime around April or May 1860, a Mr and Mrs Windle came to live at her house. By August the same year Mrs Windle had died and it was at this point that James Windle began to get very friendly with Mrs Liversedge. It seems that initially he was encouraged and certain liberties were allowed. When they went out in a party to Grimsby shortly after his wife's death, Liversedge allowed him to put his arms around her on the way home. There was a further visit to Penistone with Windle, her sister, Miss Booker and Lee Flowers, her sister's suitor. Witnesses saw her tickling his ribs when he was alone in the house with her. However it seems that her family didn't like him much and she gradually began to discourage him until he started to make threats against her and over Easter of 1861 she asked him to leave.

Eyre Street, 1910. (Reproduced courtesy of Picture Sheffield)

Liversedge also owned a small grocer's shop and Windle used to come in most days to buy bread and other items. He was a generous man who often gave her little son pennies whilst he lodged at the house. He still came back despite Liversedge having made it very clear that she would not marry him. He threatened her that if she would not have him then she would have no other and threatened to shoot her with a gun. Eventually he left her house and went to lodge nearby. Lee Flowers also lodged with her for a while and he was in the habit of leaving them talking in the kitchen whilst himself and other lodgers went to bed.

Liversedge was in the habit of sending her little son, William Henry Liversedge, to the Duke of York, a nearby pub which was owned by her sister-in-law, Hannah Booker, for a gill of beer to have with her supper. On Saturday 27 May, about 9.30 p.m., the boy went as usual to the pub, noticing Windle waiting at the top of the entry. He was served by the servant, Charlotte Oates, aged sixteen, who worked at the pub. She served the boy and he carried the pint pot carefully as he went the short distance to his house. On reaching the entry to the house he noticed Windle standing there about ten yards away. Windle asked him if a man called Johnson had been in the Duke of York, but William told him that he didn't know. With that, Windle stretched out his hand to put something in the beer. Thinking that he was going to put his hand in William pulled the pint pot away. William asked him, 'Did you put something in?' and he replied that he hadn't. Then he noticed some white powder lying on top of the beer on the foam. William was wearing an apron known as a pinafore or pinny and he wiped the powder with his pinny and went home and told his mother what had happened.

Liversedge threw the beer away and sent him for some more. When he returned to the pub to be served again, naturally Mrs Booker wanted to know why, and the child told her. Meanwhile, back home Liversedge had taken a candle to examine the pot more carefully and found some blue/green substance on the handle of the pot and some grains at the bottom. She described them as being like dust and dry and the substance on the boy's hand was also dry. At that time she did not examine the boy's apron which he had left on the sofa in the parlour. Her sister and Lee Flowers arrived and they also examined the evidence. The following day her father, Mr John Booker, arrived and advised his daughter to put some of the powder into three seperate twists of paper. Taking samples from the bottom of the pint pot and from the handle into

Postcard showing Angel Street as it was. (Reproduced courtesy of Picture Sheffield)

separate twists and also a sample from the boy's apron which now appeared to be covered by a blue/green substance. Mr Booker took the samples to Mr Weakes, a druggist of Angel Street. The following day the samples were returned and as a result of the druggist's analysis the samples were taken to the chief constable, Mr Jackson. For some unexplained reason he then took the samples home with him, possibly because the police force may have required independent corroboration, as the following day he delivered them into the hands of Dr Bingley, the Professor of Medicine at the Sheffield Medical School. The mug and the apron were delivered into the hands of Detective Officer Astey.

Windle was arrested on 29 May at his lodgings at Darnell immediately, following a diagnosis of strychnine from the medical school. Strychnine is a poison which causes anyone ingesting it to suffer muscular convulsions and eventually death in an extremely horrible manner. When charged with attempted murder on Mrs Liversedge he replied, 'Aye, so they say'. Windle was brought before the magistrate on Tuesday 4 June 1861 at the Town Hall in Sheffield. Sarah Liversedge was cross-examined over the relationship and the former closeness she had experienced with Windle. She agreed that whilst they had been close on former occasions, she had always maintained that she would never marry him. The antipathy of her parents to Windle was evident during the court hearing when Mrs Booker, her mother, uttered some vitriolic remarks about him and confirmed that her daughter had told her that she would never marry Windle on several occasions. The defence was trying to establish that the powder seen by the son, William, was tobacco as it was well-known that Windle smoked a pipe. This was challenged by the prosecution and by the son's evidence. He told the court that when he saw Windle standing in the yard that he did not have a pipe in his hand. Robert William Watson, the assistant to Mr Weakes, described the samples which he had received to examine as green/blue powder which did not resemble tobacco in any shape or form. Charlotte Oates gave her evidence, stating that the pint pot was clean when it was given to her by the boy and she emphatically stated that she did not add anything to the beer. Cross-examined, she told the court that she had drawn the beer from a pitcher which had come from a barrel in the cellars. She had also served different customers from the same pitcher and barrel. But the most damning evidence against Windle came from Dr C.F. Bingley, who told the jury that he had examined the sample on Wednesday 29 May when Detective Astey had delivered into his hands the apron and the pint pot. The powder was found to be strychnine, coloured with Prussian blue, a substance used in laundry to make white clothing look whiter. The professor went on to inform the court that on the 3 and 4 June he analyzed the substance on the pint pot and the apron, which was also found to be strychnine. The professor also gave his considered opinion that the strychnine was in the form of a solution popularly called Battles Vermin Mixture. He estimated that Windle had used about five grains of strychnine, which he believed had been more than enough to kill an adult female in very good health. A drop of substance containing $\frac{1}{200}$ part injected into a frog resulted in the death of the frog within three minutes, accompanied by the convulsions characteristic with strychnine poisoning. When questioned by the magistrate he told them that the vermin powder was for sale at any druggist or grocer and the substance was widely advertised for sale in the local newspapers of the town. When given the verdict of guilty by the jury, Windle protested his innocence stating that 'he knew nothing about it'.

The evidence against Windle was too strong and as a consequence when he appeared at the West Riding Assizes on 20 July 1861, he was found guilty of 'administering strychnine with the intention of murdering Mrs Liversedge'. His defence attempted to prove that there was simply no motive in killing her, despite the evidence that he had threatened her several times that 'if he couldn't have her no one would'. They also said that if he had used the vermin powder that he had no intention of committing a crime and was ignorant of the powerful and fatal effects that the poison would have on her. These futile attempts to escape the full retribution of the law fell on deaf ears, however, as the jury found him guilty of the crime. The judge sentenced him to life imprisonment and he was taken from the dock.

These cases were widely reported at the time in the local newspapers. Because these newspapers are preserved on fiche they are accessible to anyone interested in the subject of true crime. This book has been about murder and crime and it is inevitable that it concentrates on the seamier side of the city. Sheffield is today a prosperous, modern place which is one of eight largest cities outside London. The very pride with which it sees its industrial heritage is evident everywhere. The fogs, slums and many of the old streets and courtyards are now gone and Sheffield is a city which vibrates with night-life and shopping centres, attracting many visitors to the area. It is a safe place to live where the crime rate is low and, unlike the people in this book, its inhabitants are proud to live in a clean and healthy environment.

BIBLIOGRAPHY

Primary Sources

Sheffield Police Charge Books Ref SY/295/C7/1-9. Courtesy of Sheffield Archive Service
Map Ref Ordinance Survey Ref 294 NE 1924. Courtesy of Sheffield Local Studies Library
Map of Duke Street Ref 294.8.16 LM First Edition 1890

Secondary Sources

Sheffield & Rotherham Independent

Further Suggested Reading

Drinkall, M. (2009) *Murder and Crime in Rotherham* (The History Press: Stroud, Gloucestershire)
Bean, J. P. (1987) *Crime in Sheffield* (Sheffield City Libraries)
Bentley, D. (2002) *Sheffield Hanged 1750-1864* (ALD Design and Print)
Bentley, D. (2004) *Sheffield Murders 1865-s1965* (Lofthouse)

Other titles published by The History Press

Sheffield Shops and Shopping
RUTH HARMAN

Like most large cities, Sheffield has lost many of its family-owned shops, department stores and Co-ops over the years, and there is a strong nostalgic interest in these long-gone businesses. Illustrated with over 200 photographs and archive images, this book aims to capture the town's commercial heritage, and offers a glimps into Sheffield's past.

978 0 7524 3999 0

Haunted Sheffield
MR AND MRS P. DREADFUL

Darren Johnson-Smith, better known as Mr P. Dreadful, offers a variety of tours around Sheffield city centre each week, of which the Ghost Walk is always the most popular. This collection of stories of apparitions, manifestations, strange sightings and happenings in Sheffield's streets, churches and buildings is the perfect present for anyone with an interest in the paranormal heritage of the city.

978 0 7524 4195 5

Murder & Crime Series: Rotherham
MARGARET DRINKALL

Many of the crimes contained herein were the result of desperate poverty or an abundance of cheap gin. Some were the result of severe mental illness, such as the woman murdered because her assailant mistook her for the Devil. Some have astonishing coincidences, including the tale of the cursed watch and the two seperate murders that occurred in the same cottage. All. however, will astonish and enthrall anyone with an interest in the darker side of Rotherham's history.

978 0 7524 5424 5

Rotherham Workhouse
MARGARET DRINKALL

This fascinating volume explores all aspects of life in that dreaded institution, the workhouse. From the staff who lived and worked here to the lunatics who were kept in the medical wing, the babies and mothers whose lives began – and sometimes ended – in the maternity ward, and the destitute persons who passed through the doors every day, it reveals a side of Rotherham that has long since been forgotten. This book also contains an extensive list of workhouse inmates in Rotherham.

978 0 7524 5290 6

Visit our website and discover thousands of other History Press books.

www.thehistorypress.co.uk